BRINGING BACK OUR
TROPICAL
FORESTS

BY CAROL HAND

CONTENT CONSULTANT

Bénédicte Bachelot
Huxley Fellow
BioSciences Department
Rice University

Essential Library

An Imprint of Abdo Publishing
abdopublishing.com

CONSERVATION
SUCCESS STORIES

abdopublishing.com

Published by Abdo Publishing, a division of ABDO, PO Box 398166, Minneapolis, Minnesota 55439. Copyright © 2018 by Abdo Consulting Group, Inc. International copyrights reserved in all countries. No part of this book may be reproduced in any form without written permission from the publisher. Essential Library™ is a trademark and logo of Abdo Publishing.

Printed in the United States of America, North Mankato, Minnesota
102017
012018

THIS BOOK CONTAINS
RECYCLED MATERIALS

Cover Photo: iStockphoto
Interior Photos: Dirk Ercken/Shutterstock Images, 4; Shutterstock Images, 7, 62, 94–95, 98 (top); Felipe Trueba/UPPA/Photoshot/Newscom, 8; Jessica Wilson/NASA/Science Source, 11; Jack Chang/MCT/Newscom, 13; Dennis van de Water/Shutterstock Images, 16; Jodi Jacobson/iStockphoto, 19; Dr. Morley Read/Shutterstock Images, 20; Steve Heap/Shutterstock Images, 23; Science Source, 24–25; iStockphoto, 27, 28, 31, 35, 42, 51, 60, 68, 69, 75, 88, 99 (bottom right); Lisette van der Kroon/Shutterstock Images, 32–33, 98 (bottom); Ondrej Prosicky/Shutterstock Images, 37, 64; Tina Fields/iStockphoto, 38; Phillip Dumas/Moment/Getty Images, 41; Ton Koene/VWPics/AP Images, 44; Donal Husni/NurPhoto/Getty Images, 47; Patrick Pleul/dpa/picture-alliance/Newscom, 49, 99 (top left); Dimas Ardian/Getty Images News/Getty Images, 53; Reinhard Marscha ImageBroker/Newscom, 54; Connie Bransilver/DanitaDelimont.com Danita Delimont Photography/Newscom, 59; Bjoern Sigurdsoen/ScanPix/AP Images, 63; Michel Gunther/Science Source, 66; Henk Benglage/Shutterstock Images, 71; Ron Orman Jr./Shutterstock Images, 72–73; Martin Shield/Science Source, 77, 78, 99 (bottom left); Jonathan Alcorn/ZumaPress/Newscom, 80; Martin Harvey/NHPA/Photoshot/Newscom, 82–83; Dr. Gilbert S. Grant/Science Source, 85, 99 (top right); Mark Kostich/iStockphoto, 86; Lukas Gojda/Shutterstock Images, 90; Mark Moffett Minden Pictures/Newscom, 92; Chadamas Tuammee/Shutterstock Images, 96

Editor: Marie Pearson
Series Designer: Laura Polzin

Publisher's Cataloging-in-Publication Data

Names: Hand, Carol, author.
Title: Bringing back our tropical forests / by Carol Hand.
Description: Minneapolis, Minnesota : Abdo Publishing, 2018. | Series: Conservation success stories | Includes online resources and index.
Identifiers: LCCN 2017946791 | ISBN 9781532113161 (lib.bdg.) | ISBN 9781532152047 (ebook)
Subjects: LCSH: Rain forest conservation--Juvenile literature. | Restoration ecology--Juvenile literature. | Conservation of natural resources--Juvenile literature.
Classification: DDC 333.750--dc23
LC record available at https://lccn.loc.gov/2017946791

CONTENTS

Some animals that live in the Amazon, such as poison dart frogs, are brightly colored.

Chapter ONE

BRAZIL: A RAIN FOREST SUCCESS STORY

Entering the Amazon rain forest is like entering another world. Trees soar high above. Wide roots called buttresses spread out at a tree's base to support its straight trunk. The first branches are far above the tallest human's head. The forest canopy blocks much of the sunlight, so it is dim and cool. Streams run through and life is everywhere. Ferns, banana trees, and bromeliads abound, as do flowers and fruits. Vines hang down toward the forest floor. Brightly colored birds flit, and monkeys swing through the trees, calling and chattering. Colorful frogs, lizards, and insects appear and quickly disappear again. A lucky person might even spy a giant anaconda wrapped around a high branch, or a solitary jaguar stalking its prey. This is the undisturbed Amazon.

Brazil today is not so untouched. Swidden agriculture, or shifting cultivation, has been an agricultural practice in tropical areas for generations. Farmers clear small areas of land for short periods and then leave the land to return to forest for a longer period. These carefully nurtured regions, in which crops and forest are rotated, provide a livelihood for tropical farmers while maintaining high forest biodiversity. However, beginning in approximately the 1960s, Brazil began using a type of unsustainable swidden agriculture, usually referred to as "slash-and-burn agriculture." This term can imply that all swidden agriculture is unsustainable, however, so some avoid using it. Workers clear-cut or burn the forests to make room for cattle pastures and soybean fields. The intensity with which this practice is used has been destroying the rain forest. From 1979 to 2005, more than 200,000 square miles (500,000 sq km) of Brazilian rain forest were destroyed—an area slightly smaller than Texas. From 1996 through 2005, Brazil lost an average of 7,500 square miles (19,400 sq km) of rain forest per year. But in 2005, things began to change. Brazil's deforestation did not stop, but it declined by 70 percent between 2005 and 2014. By 2013, the

"The changes in the Brazilian Amazon in the past decade, and the contribution that they have made to slow global warming, are unprecedented."[1]

—*Doug Boucher, Pipa Elias, Jordan Faires, and Sharon Smith,* Deforestation Success Stories, *Union of Concerned Scientists, 2014*

Soy fields in Brazil cut into large areas of the Amazon rain forest.

amount lost to deforestation had declined to 2,255 square miles (5,840 sq km) per year. The country's greenhouse gas emissions dropped by 39 percent between 2005 and 2010.[2] This decrease was the greatest in history.

AMAZON DEFORESTATION AND ITS CONSEQUENCES

The Amazon rain forest extends into eight South American countries, but 60 percent of it is in Brazil.[3] Tropical rain forests are one of Earth's best defenses against global warming because they store more carbon than any other land ecosystem. This function is increasingly important as burning fossil fuel adds excess carbon dioxide to the atmosphere. Cut forests no longer absorb carbon dioxide, so deforestation causes atmospheric carbon levels to rise. Crops replacing rain forests absorb only a small percentage of the carbon

AMAZON'S INDIGENOUS TRIBES

Approximately 400 to 500 indigenous tribes live deep within the Amazon rain forest. An estimated 50 of them have no contact with the outside world.[5] The largest tribe, the Yanomami, a member of which is pictured, has approximately 22,000 members.[6] The Akuntsu tribe had only five members in 2014. Tribes harvest rain forest foods and grow crops including bananas, papayas, corn, beans, and acai berries. At least 180 languages are spoken among the tribes.[7] All tribes are threatened by deforestation, war, disease, oil development, and drug trafficking. Some protected areas safeguard indigenous tribes from these threats.

dioxide taken up by forests. Cutting the rain forests also releases the carbon stored in them, speeding up climate change.

Until the mid-1900s, Amazon deforestation was a side effect of subsistence farming. Farmers cut trees to grow cattle and food crops for their families and communities. Then, big agriculture and industry moved in, felling trees faster and faster. Large cattle ranches, soybean fields, mines, and towns replaced massive areas of forest. Roads were built through the Amazon to make it easier to cut and remove trees. By 2000, more than three-fourths of Amazon deforestation was due to cattle ranching.[4] And Brazil's deforestation rate made it the world's third-largest producer of greenhouse gases, after the United States and China.

But the Amazon provides much more than protection against global warming. Tropical forests control world climate through the water cycle. The trees release water into the atmosphere, affecting local and regional climates as well as rainfall as far away as

Central America and the western United States. The trees also suppress air pollution. The Amazon is the planet's greatest source of biodiversity, containing as much as 30 percent of all species.[8] It provides foods, medicines, and products not only to local inhabitants, but to the world. Destroying the rain forest would mean the loss of these products now and in the future. Its rivers are the area's main means of transportation, and river fish provide much of the region's protein. Many of the Amazon's indigenous tribes depend on all the rain forest has to offer. They will be displaced as the rain forest is cut.

BRAZIL GETS SERIOUS ABOUT DEFORESTATION

By the 2000s, Brazilians had begun to recognize the serious effects of deforestation. When President Luiz Inácio Lula da Silva was elected in 2002, he and his minister of the environment, Marina Silva, formed the PPCDAm (Plan for the Prevention and Combating of Deforestation in the Amazon). This program expanded Amazon protections begun by the previous president. It established protected areas, including areas for indigenous peoples, and enforced laws against illegal logging.

RUBBER TAPPERS DEFEND THE RAIN FOREST

Rubber tappers collect sap from rubber trees. This is the only source of natural rubber, and tapping is a sustainable use. Rubber tappers are also self-described guardians of the forest. These forest vigilantes take on criminal gangs who seek out old, valuable, and protected trees such as mahogany. Gang members mark the trees and come back later to cut and remove them. They export the trees, mostly to the United States. Rubber tapper and forest guardian Elizeu Berçacola says this is how illegal deforestation begins. The gangs thin the forest, decreasing biodiversity and removing seed-bearing trees. The rubber tappers patrol the forest at great risk to themselves. Sixteen were killed between 2005 and 2015.[9] Berçacola has been shot at, and his wife and children have left the state of Rondônia owing to threats.

TROPICAL FORESTS AND BIODIVERSITY

Tropical rain forests cover approximately 6 percent of Earth's surface. But they contain more than one-half of the world's plant and animal species.[10] They produce 40 percent of its oxygen. All are located in a narrow band of latitude on either side of the equator. Here, the weather remains between approximately 68 and 93 degrees Fahrenheit (20°C and 34°C) year-round. A tropical rain forest receives between 50 and 260 inches (130 to 660 cm) of rain per year. Most receive more than 100 inches (250 cm) per year.[11]

Approximately 70 percent of rain forest plants are trees. Rain forests have more kinds of trees than any other ecosystem. The trees have straight trunks that grow up to 100 feet (30 m) or more before branching.[12] At the base, the trunks spread out to form broad buttress roots that can reach 15 feet (4.6 m).[13] Rain forest trees have very shallow roots because most nutrients are near the surface. The buttresses help support the tree and increase the area through which it can obtain nutrients.

Tropical rain forests teem with life. They are the most biodiverse ecosystems on the planet. A 2.5-acre (1 ha) area of Amazon rain forest contains 100,000 insect species and 456 tree species. By contrast, the United Kingdom has only 30 native tree species. The Amazon as a whole has 40,000 species of plants—30,000 of them found only there.[14] The Amazon contains 54 percent of the total amount of rain forest left on Earth.[15] But owing to deforestation, rain forest biodiversity is declining around the world.

Tropical rain forests, shown in green, cover some areas of the globe near the equator.

For three years after da Silva's election, deforestation rose, reaching a high in 2004 and 2005. But his programs to reduce poverty and hunger were a great success. This made him popular and helped him change the attitudes of the Brazilian people. Before his presidency, people had seen deforestation as essential to development. Under da Silva, they began to see it, instead, as the wasteful destruction of Brazil's resources. In 2008, social and environmental organizations came together to form the Zero Deforestation campaign. Partners included environmental nongovernmental organizations (NGOs) such as Greenpeace, Friends of the Earth, and World Wildlife Fund (WWF). The campaign began to push back against the expanding cattle ranches and soybean farms. It directly pressured both these industries and Brazil's politicians to end deforestation.

"Civil societies pressure companies to take action and then companies pressure governments to take action."[16]

—Pipa Elias, consultant to Union of Concerned Scientists, 2014

Zero Deforestation's pressure worked. The soy industry was challenged by the 2006 Greenpeace report, *Eating Up the Amazon*. This report focused on two multinational companies, Cargill and McDonald's, which were making large profits from Amazon deforestation. The world soy industry responded quickly by declaring a moratorium on deforestation. It pledged not to buy soybeans grown on Amazon land deforested after June 24, 2006. After six years, satellite images showed the moratorium's success. A study in the Brazilian state of Mato Grosso showed that, although soy prices rose to record highs after 2007, deforestation remained very low—evidence that profits could be made without destroying the forests.

Large farms need broad areas of cleared rain forest for grazing cattle. The cattle prevent the rain forest from regrowing.

In 2009, NGOs took aim at the cattle industry. Two reports, *Time to Pay the Bill* by Amigos da Terra–Amazônia Brasileira and *Slaughtering the Amazon* by Greenpeace, described the role of cattle ranching in destroying the Amazon. Based on these reports, NGOs called for a moratorium on deforestation. Cattle ranchers resisted, but other groups—including slaughterhouses, exporters, governments, and bankers financing deforestation—agreed to the moratorium. Bankers canceled loans for expanding pastures. Supermarket chains and slaughterhouses agreed not to buy from ranchers still engaging in deforestation.

BRAZIL DECREASES DEFORESTATION

Brazil plans to decrease deforestation by 80 percent by 2020. It has made this pledge into national law and has made a strong start. Between 2001 and 2011, the nation's emission of carbon dioxide equivalents, which is a measure of total greenhouse gas releases, showed a decrease of 830 million short tons (750 million metric tons) per year. This was a cut of more than one-third, the highest of any country in the world. This success resulted entirely from a change in land use—a 64 percent decrease in deforestation for agriculture.[18] Other sectors of the economy, including energy, agriculture, industry, and waste production, all increased their greenhouse gas emissions.

The moratoria were voluntary, but in some states, they were enforced legally. The cattle industry has changed much more slowly than the soy industry, but deforestation has declined. Progress is being made.

In 2015, Brazilian President Dilma Rousseff and President Barack Obama entered an agreement designed to combat climate change. Among other features, Brazil agreed to a reforestation project— restoring a 30-million-acre (12 million ha) region of forest, an area approximately the size of Pennsylvania.[17] Because both countries changed administrations in 2016 and 2017, the future of this agreement is unclear, but it signals Brazil's continued interest in maintaining its rain forest.

AMAZON REGION PROTECTED AREAS

Brazil showed a decade of record-breaking slowdowns in deforestation, but it will be hard to keep up this momentum. To make sure the Brazilian Amazon remains protected forever, several groups cooperated to form the Amazon Region Protected Areas (ARPA) project. Launched in 2002, ARPA's goal is to turn 150 million acres (61 million ha) of the Brazilian Amazon forest into two types of areas, some strictly protected and others open to sustainable use. By 2014, ARPA had successfully designated 100 different sites, together making an area the size of California.

According to Carter Roberts, president and chief executive officer (CEO) of WWF, "There's nothing bigger than ARPA. It's the biggest conservation project of all time." The next phase, ARPA for Life, will extend into the future. ARPA for Life will make sure all protected areas remain permanently protected. Its partners have created a $215 million transition fund.[19] This fund will help Brazil maintain the areas until its own economy is strong and stable enough to sustain them by itself. ARPA's continued success flows from the involvement of many groups and from its innovative financing. ARPA hopes to become a model of conservation around the world.

Brazil's impressive decade of slowed deforestation stems from two major factors. First, the attitude of the Brazilian people changed as they began to see deforestation as a threat to their future and a waste of valuable resources. Second, many groups of people closely cooperated, including individuals, NGOs, the Brazilian government, and many international partners. A combination of pressure on offending industries and dedication to establishing protected areas gives hope that other countries can experience similar successes.

REDD SAVES RAIN FORESTS

The United Nations (UN) has created a mechanism for slowing tropical deforestation. Known as REDD (Reducing Emissions from Deforestation and Degradation), the program is designed to assign a dollar value to carbon storage. A country gains carbon credits by decreasing deforestation, and international donors pay the country for the credits. This gives developing countries an incentive to reduce deforestation. The newer REDD+ initiative adds conservation of biodiversity, sustainable forest management, and improvement of local livelihoods to its goals. Brazil is one of several Amazon countries using REDD in its Amazon protection program.

El Yunque National Forest in Puerto Rico is the only tropical rain forest in the United States.

THE VALUE AND THE THREAT

Tropical rain forests are vital to the existence of life on Earth, beginning with their effect on global weather and climate. Tropical forests include tropical mountain systems, tropical moist forests, tropical rain forests, and tropical dry forests. They also include tropical savanna woodlands, which are open and not dense, and mangroves with trees that grow along the coasts. All rain forests help control Earth's temperature by pulling carbon dioxide, a greenhouse gas, out of the atmosphere during photosynthesis. The Center for Global Development in Washington, DC, predicts that, by 2050, deforestation will have destroyed 714 million acres (289 million ha) of tropical forests. If this much forest is cut, an additional

186 billion short tons (169 billion metric tons) of carbon dioxide will enter the atmosphere by 2050. This is the same as the amount made by 44,000 coal-fired power plants running for a year.[1] To decrease the rate of climate change, deforestation must be reversed.

RAIN FOREST VALUES

Rain forests also control the water cycle. Trees pull water into their roots and then upward and out into the atmosphere, where it forms clouds. Rain falls from the clouds, which completes the water cycle and strongly influences regional climate. But the influence of rain forests does not stay within the region. Moisture in the atmosphere moves by wind currents around Earth. Cutting trees in the Amazon affects weather in the western United States. Deforestation in Central Africa affects precipitation in the US Midwest. Tree loss in Southeast Asia affects precipitation in China and the Balkan Peninsula. Rain entering rivers and oceans influences ocean circulation. Ocean circulation moves water around the ocean, and the temperature of that water influences air temperatures.

As the world's most biodiverse ecosystem, rain forests provide habitat for an estimated 30 million

HOW DEFORESTATION COULD AFFECT AMERICAN WEATHER

Amazon deforestation results from cutting trees for agriculture and industry, but as climate changes, temperature increases and drying could destroy up to 85 percent of the forest. Researchers at Princeton University and the University of Miami studied the potential effect of Amazon deforestation on US climate. Their model shows that wind patterns would move drying Amazon air over the western United States from December to February. A treeless Amazon would cause 20 percent less rain in the coastal Northwest—now a temperate rain forest—and a 50 percent smaller Sierra Nevada snowpack, supplying less water for Californian cities and farms.[2] Complete loss of the Amazon is unlikely, but even small losses will affect these climates.

species of plants and animals—two-thirds of Earth's plant species and one-half of its animals.[3] This includes one-third of all birds and 90 percent of all invertebrates.[4] Ecologists estimate that millions of species of rain forest plants, insects, and microorganisms have not even been discovered. Thus, their value to the rain forest—and to humans—is unknown. As rain forests are destroyed, scientists estimate that approximately 50,000 species per year (137 per day) are being lost.[5]

An often-overlooked ecosystem function of rain forests is to prevent flooding, erosion, and siltation, which is the buildup of loose particles swept along by running water. Like all vegetation, rain forest trees hold soil in place. The heavy canopy protects the ground from the impact of heavy rains, and water runs down the trunks, reaching the ground in a slow, gentle flow. The trees themselves store massive amounts of water, slowing runoff and erosion. When the trees are cut, these functions are lost. Heavy rains hit the bare soil directly, increasing floods, erosion, and siltation of

SECRET LIFE OF A RAIN FOREST TREE

In the early 1990s, *Life* magazine asked environmental photographer Gary Braasch to illustrate the richness of tropical forests. Braasch lived in and photographed life in a single 200-foot tree in a remote part of a Costa Rican wilderness preserve. For three weeks, he lived on or near a simple platform and slept in a hammock in the tree's canopy, 150 feet (46 m) above ground. From his high perch, Braasch saw the sun, felt cool breezes, and was drenched by daily tropical downpours. He lived among spider and howler monkeys, pictured, swinging through branches, raucous cries of macaws and parrots, and tiny birds and insects flitting among tree limbs coated with mosses, ferns, and orchids. He photographed it all: 4,500 pictures, a tiny microcosm of the rain forest's massive biodiversity.[6]

Roots keep floodwater from washing away soil.

rivers. Increased flooding in areas such as Bangladesh, Thailand, and the Philippines is a direct result of deforestation.

Finally, rain forests serve as the world's pharmacy and grocery store. Of current modern medicines, at least 25 percent originated in a rain forest.[7] These include treatments for leukemia, malaria, high blood pressure, and mental illness, among others. Yet scientists estimate only 1 percent of rain forest plants have so far been studied to determine their medical potential. Eighty percent of diets in developed countries originated in the rain forest. Anyone who buys nuts, coffee, cocoa, or spices is buying a rain forest product. Fruits including bananas, coconuts, avocados, figs, mangoes, tomatoes, and citrus fruits all come from the rain forest. Three thousand fruits originate in the rain forest.[8] These fruits are just a small portion of its 75,000 edible plants.[9] Rain forests are the source of rubber, resins, and fibers. Many foods and other products are likely yet undiscovered.

THREATS TO RAIN FORESTS

Rain forests once covered 14 percent of Earth's surface; in the 2010s, they covered only 6 percent.[10] They are being rapidly deforested for agriculture, logging, cattle ranching, mining, oil production, and dam construction. Half of Earth's rain forests were destroyed between the early 1900s and early 2000s.[11] At present destruction rates, they could all be gone by 2117.

Up to 50 percent of tropical forests are being destroyed, mostly to provide grazing and plantation lands.[12] In the Amazon, cattle ranching is responsible for as much as 80 percent of rain forest destruction.[13]

RAIN FORESTS, WEST AND EAST

Western Hemisphere rain forests occur in Central America and the Amazon basin. Eastern Hemisphere forests include two separate areas: African forests in the Congo, West Africa, and Madagascar; and regions of Southeast Asia, including small regions of New Guinea and Australia. Each region has its own unique species. The Amazon has the highest levels of biodiversity, Southeast Asia the second highest, and Africa the lowest. The Amazon is the largest rain forest. Central Africa is second, with many high-altitude cloud forests. Bangladesh, in Southeast Asia, has the world's largest concentration of mangrove forests. Australia's rain forests have dense, lush understory growth due to wet Pacific winds.

Cattle ranches provide low-cost beef to people in North America, China, and Russia. It takes an estimated 200 square feet (19 sq m) of rain forest to produce a single pound of beef.[14] But the pastures don't last. Most of the regions' nutrients are in the trees, not the soil, and they are lost when the trees are removed. Without trees, the soil erodes and dries out, causing desert conditions within a few years. Ranchers move on, destroying a new area. Rain forests are also replaced with huge plantations of palm oil, sugarcane, coffee, tea, bananas, pineapples, and other crops. These large plantations are often unsustainable. When the land becomes unproductive, the farmers move on, cutting more forest.

"Destroying rain forest for economic gain . . . is like burning a Renaissance painting to cook a meal."[15]

—Biologist E. O. Wilson, 1990

Logging in the rain forest is another big business. Specific trees, such as mahogany and ebony, are cut and sold as lumber for making fine furniture, building materials, and even coffins, which are immediately buried or burned. Other trees are cut to make paper and charcoal. Logging cannot happen without building roads and using heavy machinery. This destroys even more forest.

Increasingly, materials such as aluminum, gold, copper, and diamonds are being mined from rain forests. Mining destroys trees and causes erosion. It also uses toxic chemicals such as mercury, which enter streams and rivers, poisoning organisms. Oil industries explore for new oil deposits, build roads and pipelines, and cause oil spills that poison forest life. Industries that remove rain forest products are highly unsustainable. They are short-term boom industries. Workers move in, form settlements, and cause rampant forest destruction.

Some people grow mahogany trees to harvest the wood.

Poor people from surrounding areas enter the settlements and clear more forest for subsistence farming. The resource is quickly depleted, and the workers move on, leaving behind a devastated forest and a community with few economic options.

In developing countries, hydroelectric dams are being built to produce electricity. Many trees are removed, often by illegal logging. The dams flood large areas, destroying more forest. But forest dams are usually short-lived because the submerged trees acidify the water as they rot, corroding the dam's turbines.

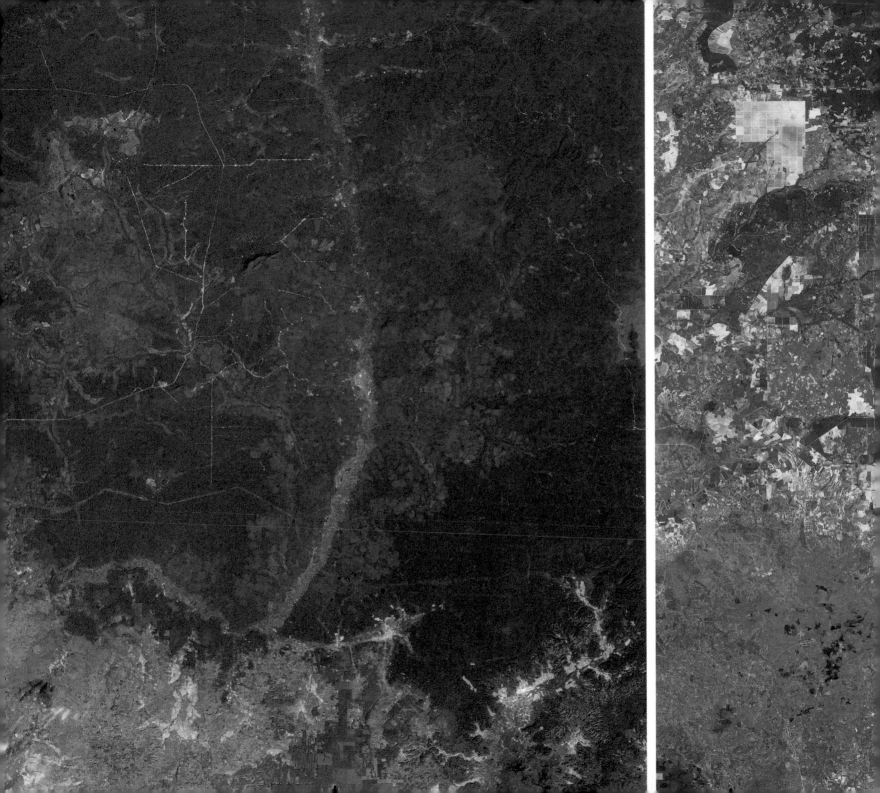

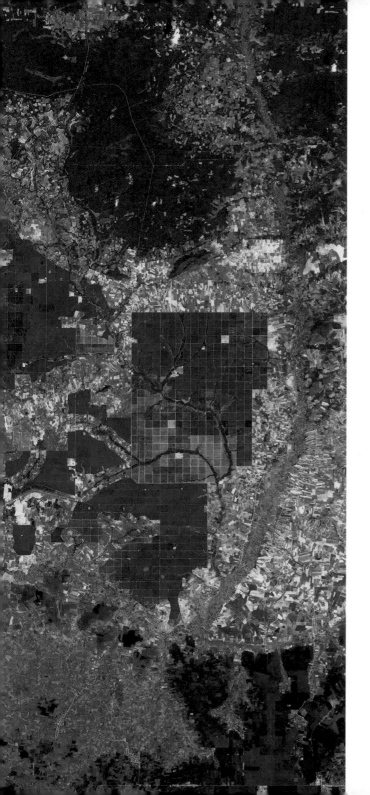

Rain forest destruction often results in forest fragmentation. The forest—once an unbroken mass of trees—is cut up into small fragments surrounded by soy fields or pastures or crisscrossed by roads or power lines. The trees around the edges of fragments are subjected to hot winds, which knock them down or cause heat stress. These trees die three times faster than trees inside an untouched forest. This makes the forest unstable. The massive trees common in the forest interior are lost in fragmented habitats.

Fragmentation also disrupts wildlife movement and breeding patterns. Weeds and feral animals invade. Remaining wildlife no longer has the rich food supply available in the intact forest. Larger predators venture into pastures and other human settlements, killing livestock and causing humans to kill them. As native species die out, they leave unused resources, which non-native species can use. These species

Satellite images show a Cambodian rain forest as it was in 2000, *left*, and how it appeared in 2015, fragmented by rubber plantations, logging, and agricultural fields.

may become invasive and further disrupt the ecosystem. In the Western Ghats, a highly biodiverse region of India, plant invaders include coffee, tea, and *Eucalyptus*.

For thousands of years, indigenous peoples have called the rain forests home. Now, as the developed world destroys their homes for profit, indigenous peoples are being driven out. They lose their homes, foods, medicines, and ways of life. They succumb to diseases brought in by outsiders exploiting the forests. The Awá, an indigenous Amazon hunter-gatherer tribe, has only 355 surviving members; 100 of them have never seen the outside world. They are being attacked and massacred by gunmen, illegal loggers, and ranchers. Their camps are destroyed by logging equipment, and logging itself destroys the forest, on which they depend for everything. According to Fiona Watson of Survival International, "It is not just the destruction of the land; it is the violence. . . . This is extinction taking place before our eyes."[16] As indigenous peoples die out, their knowledge of rain forest life is being lost. Medicine men, especially, have centuries of accumulated knowledge of the medicinal uses of rain forest plants.

"Each time a rainforest medicine man dies, it is as if a library has burned down."[17]

—Leslie Taylor, in The Healing Power of Rainforest Herbs

This and other cultural information is lost as the younger generations of indigenous peoples, attracted to the wealth and technology of the outside world, leave rather than learn and pass on the knowledge of their ancestors.

As human populations grow, threats to rain forests are becoming more serious. In developing countries, cutting the forests may be the locals' only option for food and fuel.

Some organizations protect
certain species from poaching.
The Douc Langur Foundation
monitors douc langurs and
removes traps that might harm
the primates.

INDONESIA'S ENDANGERED SPECIES

Indonesia has one of the world's richest, most biodiverse rain forests. Its forests are spread across 18,000 islands, encompassing 1 percent of Earth's land area. Indonesia contains 12 percent of all mammal species but also has more endangered mammals than any other country—135 species, or one-third of its native mammals.[18] The Sumatran tiger, Javan rhinoceros, Sumatran elephant, and orangutan, pictured, are all critically endangered. This is the highest category on the International Union for Conservation of Nature and Natural Resources (IUCN) Red List of Threatened Species. It means the species faces an extremely high risk of extinction in the wild.

Forestland is often free to those who clear and settle it. As open-access or common property, rain forests can be exploited by anyone, such as a local farmer or outside industrialist. There is no incentive for conservation. There is competition to take advantage of the resource before someone else does. This is an example of the "tragedy of the commons," where an easily available or commonly owned resource is depleted because each person acts for his or her own advantage, rather than for the well-being of the whole society or ecosystem.

Deforestation greatly harms rain forest ecosystems. But hunters are also a large threat. They may be the most significant threat to rain forest biodiversity in Southeast Asia. Forests are now nearly empty of large vertebrates, including tigers, rhinoceroses, elephants, bears, and langurs. These species are often sold for single body parts such as skins or tusks. Pigs and rats are often hunted for meat. Hunting is increasing due to better access to forests by road, better weapons, and higher demand for wildlife as pets, meat, and medicines. As large vertebrates decrease, hunters target smaller species, including songbirds. Others use nonspecific weapons such as snares and shotguns. These may capture or kill species that aren't targeted. Throughout the region, hunting is rampant and unsustainable. Overhunting certain species disrupts the way an ecosystem works. This can make it harder for other animals and plants to survive.

Usually, rain forest management includes a mixture of conservation and preservation. Conservation maximizes the well-being of natural biodiversity, human health, and human safety. It involves managing public lands to keep them sustainable while still allowing people to use them responsibly. Land use must not destroy local ecosystems but keep them functional for many generations. Preservation requires land to be kept in its natural form, without extraction or exploitation of resources. Rain forest management might involve preservation of some rain forests in wilderness preserves or national parks. Others might be managed for careful, sustainable uses. Proper management always involves stopping or significantly slowing deforestation, plus reforestation where needed. No single magic bullet will make these changes possible. Governments, NGOs, and individuals working together can change public attitudes, emphasize community involvement, and develop workable laws to save the world's rain forests.

THE VERTICAL RAIN FOREST

The four layers of a tropical rain forest are like four different worlds. The topmost, or emergent, layer consists of tall trees. They are far apart and anywhere from 100 to 240 feet (30 to 73 m) tall.[19] They are exposed to all weather extremes, from hot tropical sun to winds to rainstorms. Their environment is bright and changeable. Many animals in the emergent layer are fliers, such as the predatory harpy eagle.

Directly below the emergent layer is the dense canopy, home to most of the rain forest's life. It extends approximately 60 to 130 feet (18 to 40 m) above the ground and acts as a leaky roof over the rest of the forest.[20] Many branches are covered with woody vines or plants that grow directly on other plants. Inside the canopy, it is darker and much more humid than in the emergent layer. Many trees produce fruits that provide food for monkeys, birds, and other canopy animals.

The third layer down is the understory. Typical understory trees tend to be approximately 60 feet (18 m) tall.[21] The understory is relatively dark, with only 2 to 15 percent of the light in the canopy.[22] Young trees, small trees, and shrubs grow here. Many animals are camouflaged, either for protection or to help catch food. The understory is more open than the canopy and has many fliers, including bats and birds.

The forest floor receives less than 2 percent of the canopy light.[23] Detritus from above collects here and decomposes. Fungi and small invertebrates—centipedes, slugs, and beetles—feed on the decaying matter. Underground roots provide a rich food source for some animals. Many large animals travel the forest floor. These include tapirs and jaguars in the Amazon, tigers and Asian elephants in Asia, and leopards, elephants, and gorillas in Africa.

Emergent layer

Canopy layer

Understory layer

Forest floor

Different species are adapted to live in certain levels of the rain forest.

Logging is one of the biggest threats to the rain forest on the island of Borneo.

Chapter THREE

SAVING FORESTS BY SAVING PEOPLE

Most rain forests exist in poor countries where people depend on forest resources for survival. Forests are mainly destroyed by industrial activities such as logging, cattle ranches, and commercial agriculture. There are economic incentives for these activities, but few incentives exist for preserving the rain forest. Successful rain forest conservation can only occur when the local people's needs and the country's needs are met. Short-term needs must be balanced with long-term benefits produced by conservation and sustainable use of the rain forest.

FOOD SECURITY

Africa contains approximately 30 percent of the world's rain forests. In West Africa, much of this land has been cleared for farming since the 1980s. Much of the Congo basin is still untouched, but as populations grow, deforestation will likely rise, says Yadvinder Malhi, director of Oxford University's Center for Tropical Forests. But this could be avoided. "You could have the current agricultural output of the Africa tropical forest region in 40 percent of its current agricultural land," Malhi says, "leaving 60 percent of the land available for forests if the agriculture was intensified."[1]

"Rainforests will only continue to survive as functional ecosystems if they can be shown to provide tangible economic benefits."[2]

—Rhett Butler, founder of Mongabay and cofounder of the journal Tropical Conservation Science

Brazil showed that it was possible to both feed people and save rain forests. President da Silva began his administration in 2003 by fighting poverty and hunger. Only after these programs began to succeed did he tackle deforestation. But both can be done at once. Certain cultivation techniques improve soils while supplying food and saving forests. Permaculture is a sustainable form of agriculture that relies on techniques used in nature, including growing a mixture of crops together. This returns nutrients to the soil while increasing food variety and economic stability. A technique derived from Amazon societies involves fertilizing soil with charcoal

The Congo basin supports many species, including forest elephants.

THE POWER OF THE INGA TREE

Growing food in the rain forest is difficult due to its poor soil. In the past, people cleared a new garden patch every year, but this destroys the forest. Now, some Amazonian people use the inga tree to replenish soil nutrients. They plant rows of inga saplings in a food garden, forming an alley. The fast-growing saplings form a shady canopy over the alley. They pull nitrogen from the air. Gardeners prune small branches and leaves from the trees and scatter them in the alley, where they rot, releasing nutritious nitrogen. Their crops grow up and absorb the nitrogen. After harvest, inga trees continue to grow. This cycle can continue for many years, growing food while preserving the forest.

and animal bones. The resulting soil is called *terra preta*, or biochar. This provides better crops and stores carbon in the soil, decreasing climate change. Another form of sustainable agriculture is traditional swidden agriculture. In this method, an area is cleared and planted for a short time and then left untouched for a long period so the forest can return.

Economic incentives that help improve conditions for subsistence farmers can indirectly benefit rain forests. Governments can help poor farmers gain formal ownership rights to their land. This would give them incentive to improve their land, instead of clearing more forest. Working with microcredit companies would allow poor farmers to both save and borrow money, increasing financial security and promoting entrepreneurship. Finally, better access to markets would improve farmers' finances. But this access should be carefully planned so building roads and other infrastructure does not destroy more forest.

FIGHTING CLIMATE CHANGE

Saving forests has also come to mean fighting climate change. Forests, economies, and people are increasingly threatened by changes brought on by the warming climate.

Deforestation and forest degradation increase the amount of greenhouse gases being released into the atmosphere. Thus, work to save forests often includes reducing carbon emissions. These initiatives usually involve the cooperation of many groups. Community efforts, where people have a stake in deciding their own futures, are among the most important.

Mexico is a leader in fighting climate change. It committed to cutting its global warming emissions to half of its 2000 level by 2050 through using several methods. A major achievement is the Payment for Environmental Services program (PSA), in which users of ecosystem services such as clean water and biodiversity are expected to pay providers of those services. The providers maintain healthy ecosystems and prevent deforestation. They may build firebreaks, control pests and diseases, prevent illegal logging and poaching, and maintain clean water supplies. PSA payments give an incentive for forest conservation and help change attitudes of communities toward natural resources.

BIRDS CONNECT TROPICAL AND TEMPERATE ZONES

Despite their small land area, Central American rain forests have more bird species than all of North America. Panama alone has 700 species, including the golden-hooded tanager, pictured. But this is changing as the forests disappear. In 1950, Central America was 60 percent forest; by 1980, this figure had dropped to 41 percent.[3] El Salvador has almost no forest left. This loss is felt in North America. Many migrating birds, such as the wood thrush and the Tennessee warbler, winter in Central or South America. As their habitats are destroyed, their populations decline.

HOW CHOCOLATE SAVES RAIN FOREST PEOPLE

The Asháninka people live in Peru's Ene River valley, a remote Amazon region threatened by illegal logging and the coca trade. Working with Cool Earth, a UK charity, the Asháninka cultivate and sell criollo, the world's most highly valued cacao bean. Its production is now the main source of income for 174 families. Cool Earth provides tools, seedlings, and a cacao technician. It ships harvested cacao beans to Cornwall, United Kingdom, where they are made into chocolate bars. Sergio Capeshi, president of the local cacao cooperative, says, "What I love most . . . is being able to support my Asháninka brothers. Cacao is vital for us. It gives a household sustainability—money for health, education, food for our children."[4]

When the PSA began in 2003 and 2004, the Mexican government was to make payments with loans from the World Bank. Later, private consumers would take over as world markets based on carbon storage developed. But world carbon markets have not developed, and the government is still paying. However, the program is considered a partial success. Nearly all PSA sites are investing much of their payments in forest management. This is reducing the rate of deforestation, which lowers greenhouse gas emissions and benefits rural and indigenous peoples.

Like Mexico, Costa Rica has a strong record in fighting climate change and protecting biodiversity. It has expanded its protected forest areas, paid for ecosystem services, and promoted ecotourism. These methods have transformed the Costa Rican people's attitudes toward protecting the environment. The country has embraced the idea of carbon neutrality—achieving a net-zero carbon footprint by removing as much carbon from the atmosphere as residents add to it. Carbon neutrality slows or stops human-caused global warming. Costa Rica has combined reversing deforestation with improvements in its people's social and economic development. Since the 2000s, deforestation of rain forests on its Caribbean coast has been reversed.

COMMUNITY INVOLVEMENT

One of the most successful types of projects in preventing deforestation has been the use of community management. That is, rather than federal governments telling communities how to manage their forests, each community develops and carries out its own plan. Often in such plans, groups of communities work together. Each develops a plan that fits its needs, but all work together toward a common goal—preventing deforestation and decreasing carbon pollution.

Madagascar, an island off the coast of southeastern Africa, is combining government action with community involvement. Madagascar is known for its rare and exotic plants and animals, but deforestation has decimated many species. Beginning in 2003, the government gave partial protection to a wide corridor of land in southeastern Madagascar. This corridor supported cattle grazing and timber cutting, as well as plantations of rice, coffee, and bananas. It connected already protected areas in the lowlands and highlands.

Cooperating groups within the Madagascar corridor designated protected areas, sustainable-use forests, and settlements. They used community management to improve the region's economy. Project managers came from within the community, not from outside. The cooperating groups provided grants for farmers to develop sustainable agricultural practices, such as tree nurseries, ecotourism and agroforestry, or growing trees or shrubs among crops or pastureland. Success in decreasing deforestation was measured by reduced greenhouse gas emissions. The region reduced carbon dioxide emissions by 2.4 million short tons (2.2 million metric tons) between 2007 and 2012.[5] Groups also developed programs for health services, including nutrition, hygiene, water, sanitation, and family planning.

India is also trying to save its forests through community action. For more than 150 years, its forests were exploited and destroyed, usually for agriculture. In the 1990s, the 1988 National Forest Policy Act began to reverse this trend by prioritizing forest conservation over economic benefit. The act gave control of forests to cooperative community groups in individual Indian states. The country now has 106,000 cooperating villages, one of the world's largest community forest projects.[6] Each village works with its state's forest department to create its own plan. It receives a share of the income from products harvested in its area. Local enforcers control illegal logging, fires, and poaching.

Programs in Madagascar give locals jobs growing and planting rain forest trees.

But much of India's recent reforestation is due to tree plantations rather than the growth of natural forests. Also, many forests are still being degraded as local residents cut trees for fuelwood. A new plan, Mission for a Green India (GIM) will operate between

Some poachers in India target tigers.

2012 and 2022. It will add 12 million acres (5 million ha) of new forest and restore another 12 million acres by 2022.[8] GIM's goal is to decrease India's contribution to carbon dioxide emissions and global warming.

COMMUNITY RIGHTS

Mexico and Central America have a long tradition of recognizing the rights of indigenous peoples and local communities. Sixty-five percent of their forests legally belong to these groups, compared with 30 percent in Asia.[9] But these rights are conflicting with the preservation of biodiversity. Beginning with US national parks in the 1800s, indigenous peoples and local communities have often been forced to move when conservation areas are set up. They have lost their rights to the land. Overcoming this problem requires listening to indigenous peoples and involving them in forest protection.

Andrew Davis of the PRISMA Foundation, an El Salvador environmental group, advocates a rights-based approach to conserving forests. He points out that many community groups and indigenous peoples are committed to sustainable use of their environments, and they are capable of creating and running enterprises that promote these uses. For example, Alimentos Nutri-Naturales (ANSA), a company formed by three Guatemalan women in 2005, harvests and sells Maya nuts from the buffer zone of the Maya Biosphere Reserve. This keeps more trees standing in the buffer zone while providing jobs for 180 people in the region. Successes such as these show that community rights are key to preserving tropical forests.

"When you recognize rights and invest in these organizations [then] you can have enterprises that conserve biodiversity and also contribute to the development of the population."[10]

—Andrew Davis, senior researcher,
PRISMA Foundation

While Brazil's deforestation was slowing in the 2000s, farmers grew trees to help replant parts of the Amazon.

FOUR

SLOWING OR STOPPING DEFORESTATION

Rain forests around the world are being deforested. Since the 1990s, most destruction has occurred in the tropics of Africa and South America. Between 1990 and 2010, deforestation in Africa was much higher in Madagascar and West Africa than in the Congo. Southeast Asia lost 14.5 percent of its forest from 2000 to 2017, including more than half of its old-growth forests. Some parts of Indonesia may lose 98 percent of their forests by 2022.[1] After a highly successful "save the rain forest" movement in the 2000s, Brazil's deforestation rates rose in 2015 for the first time in almost a decade. Sustaining good management and protecting forests is important to keeping rain forests healthy well into the future.

Deforestation causes a loss of trees equivalent in size to 36 football fields every minute.[5]

Southeast Asia demonstrates the many dangers threatening rain forests. A major driver of deforestation is agriculture—especially plantations for rubber, palm oil, and pulp and paper. The region supplies almost 90 percent of the world's palm oil and paper. Dam construction is also eating up rain forests; 78 new dams were planned in the Mekong delta as of 2017.[2] This construction will lead to massive loss of freshwater biodiversity, flooding, and regional droughts. Although deforestation is occurring in many places, projects are underway to stop it.

MAKING PALM OIL SUSTAINABLE

The snack food industry's use of palm oil is a major cause of rain forest destruction and is significantly increasing carbon emissions and global warming. Palm oil is produced from oil palms native to Africa. As of 2016, there were many palm oil plantations in Indonesia and Malaysia, and they were expanding to Central and West Africa and Latin America. Plantations have replaced 37 million acres (15 million ha) of rain forest land.[3] Rainforest Action Network (RAN) coined the term *conflict palm oil* to describe oil produced on plantations created by rain forest destruction. Approximately one-half of packaged foods in the United States contain conflict palm oil, and demand is increasing rapidly.[4]

Some responsible palm oil companies work to conserve the forests on their lands.

RAN, among other groups, is pressuring the Snack Food 20—or 20 of the world's largest food companies—to use only responsibly produced palm oil. In 2014, some, including Kellogg's, Mars, Hershey's, and General Mills, agreed not to buy conflict palm oil. This is a partial solution. But other companies, including PepsiCo, have not made this pledge. Some people want to boycott companies that have not made the pledge, but boycotts do not always work. Another solution would be for the countries involved to regulate the industry, but because of the huge profits in palm oil, they are often reluctant to do so.

In 2003, palm oil companies themselves began efforts to make the industry more sustainable. The Roundtable on Sustainable Palm Oil (RSPO) develops criteria for

SELECTIVE LOGGING OR PLANTATIONS?

In Southeast Asia, the remaining virgin forest is mostly protected in nature reserves. The rest has been either destroyed or selectively logged. In selectively logged forests, the largest and most valuable trees are cut, and the area is left to regenerate. Thirty to 50 years later, the process is repeated. Selective logging can be sustainable. But some selective loggers remove the largest, strongest trees, leaving the weakest to reproduce. The logging damages surrounding trees and the network of vines connecting them, decreasing forest stability. Regrowth is slower in selectively logged areas because less sunlight reaches the forest floor than in clear-cut areas. Sustainable selectively logged and virgin forest are both valuable for wildlife. But palm oil plantations make much more money than logging projects, so they are rapidly displacing forests. In Kalimantan, Indonesia, between 1990 and 2010, 90 percent of the land used to establish palm oil plantations had been forested.[7] Plantations are extremely poor habitats for wildlife. They further lower biodiversity by fragmenting the remaining forest, preventing wildlife from moving between habitats.

sustainable production and helps companies adopt these practices. But the environmental organization Greenpeace points to RSPO companies that are continuing rapid deforestation. Greenpeace favors a halt on deforestation throughout Indonesia until more-effective procedures can be developed.

The Rainforest Alliance is helping palm oil production turn toward sustainability. In 2008, this NGO began working with farmers and businesses. It certifies farms that carry out sustainable practices, such as maintaining healthy soil, protecting waterways, reducing and recycling waste, and reducing or eliminating use of pesticides. Farmers must also protect natural habitats and wildlife. For example, certified farmers cannot cut most forests, which provide habitat for endangered species such as orangutans. First to receive certification was a group of 600 Honduran farmers. Overall, approximately 6.5 million farmers, including 3 million small farmers, depend on palm oil for their livelihoods.[6] So far, the

Rainforest Alliance sustainability program is operating in Colombia, Costa Rica, Guatemala, Honduras, Indonesia, and Papua New Guinea.

PREVENTING LEAKAGE

Sometimes deforestation slows in one country but increases in a nearby country. This is known as global leakage. It may also increase beside a protected rain forest. This is local leakage. When leakage happens, the world's net deforestation has not decreased, but deforestation has simply moved, and no progress has been made. The small country of Guyana, in northeastern South America, hopes to avoid becoming a victim of global leakage. Guyana is a high-forest, low-deforestation (HFLD) country; it is almost 87 percent forest and, so far, has had almost no deforestation (approximately 0.03 percent per year from 2000 to 2009).[8] This places Guyana at high risk for future deforestation. Industries are likely to move in from countries such as neighboring Brazil, where forests have already been overharvested. To stave off leakage, Guyana

The Rainforest Alliance certifies produce that was sustainably farmed.

is partnering with Norway to develop economically without increasing deforestation rates. Success equals low carbon emissions coupled with growth. When Guyana demonstrates success, Norway makes payments. Guyana uses the payments for low-carbon development projects and awards land titles to its indigenous communities.

The Congo basin, another HFLD region, is responsible for 90 percent of Africa's carbon storage. It is a major contributor to reducing global warming. Congo basin countries hope to keep deforestation rates low and prevent global leakage of deforestation. So far, success is high—deforestation, already low, declined by one-half in the 1990s and 2000s.[9]

FOREST OR SUPERHIGHWAY?

The Ekuri people of Nigeria are fighting for their forests and their livelihoods. Their governor seized a massive corridor of rain forest to build a superhighway. The corridor, 12.4 miles (20 km) wide and 160 miles (260 km) long, crosses several protected areas, including a national park.[10] Conservationists feared the governor planned to open the area to timber companies, also giving illegal loggers and poachers easy access to the forest. As of February 2017, thanks to the Ekuri people's protests, the governor returned the corridor to the community. But the fight is not over. He did not cancel the superhighway project, and forest clearing might soon begin. The Ekuri vow to fight until the project is canceled.

As elsewhere, Congo's success is the result of a combination of factors. Agriculture, the main driver of deforestation in Asia and the Amazon, is less important there. Much of the Congo rain forest is inaccessible. It is thick jungle with few roads and people. Africa's abundant savanna, which is far easier to convert to cropland, has been exploited for agriculture instead. Development of the oil and gas industries has led to higher incomes, greater urbanization, and more food imports, causing agriculture to decline even more. And only large cities have a demand for fuelwood and charcoal. Most rain forests, which are far from cities, are left untouched.

Beginning in the 1990s, all Congo basin countries established forest protection programs. The programs grew throughout the 2000s. The largest of these programs, the Congo Basin Forest Partnership (CBFP), consists of 21 governments, 12 international organizations, 20 nonprofit groups, and eight private sector organizations. It protects 13 conservation regions that include key ecological zones and biodiversity hot spots.[11] According to a 2013 report by the United Nations (UN) Food and Agriculture Organization (FAO), these sustainable production–forest management programs are gradually replacing intensive logging.

The routes to curbing deforestation are many, and they vary according to the needs of each region. Almost always, they require a combination of measures and many people working together. But whatever the measures, stopping deforestation is a priority for combating global warming, saving Earth's biodiversity, and improving the lives of indigenous peoples.

THE COST OF DEFORESTATION

The Congo basin contains the world's second-largest rain forest. At 500 million acres (200 million ha), it is larger than Alaska. It spans six countries and provides food and shelter to 75 million people from 150 ethnic groups. Many are hunter-gatherers who live in and depend entirely on the rain forest. The Congo basin teems with plant and animal life. Thirty percent of its approximately 10,000 plant species are unique to the Congo. It supports more than 400 species of mammals, 1,000 bird species, and 700 fish species.[12] Many familiar Congo mammals—including elephants, chimpanzees, mountain gorillas, and bonobos, pictured—are endangered. If deforestation continues, they may go extinct.

TROPICAL PEATLAND FORESTS

The soils of tropical peatland forests remain waterlogged all year. These soils are very low in oxygen. They slow decomposition and produce peat, a soil made of partly decomposed plant debris. As of 2011, Southeast Asia was thought to comprise approximately 56 percent of the world's total peatland forests.[13] These forests are found primarily on the islands of Sumatra, Borneo, and New Guinea. But in 2012, two scientists, Professor Simon Lewis and Dr. Greta Dargie, both from the University of Leeds and University College London, discovered a large region of peatland in the Congo basin. This region, the Cuvette Centrale peatlands, covers more than 56,200 square miles (145,500 sq km), an area larger than England.[14]

Peatland forests are major carbon sinks. Peat soils store more carbon than soils in any other type of tropical forest—five to ten times more than upland tropical rain forests.[15] The Cuvette Centrale peatland covers only 4 percent of the Congo basin, but it is one of the world's most carbon-rich ecosystems. Its soil stores as much carbon as the amount stored in the trees covering the other 96 percent of the forest.[16]

Carbon storage makes peatland forests important tools in the world's fight against climate change. But if peatland soils dry out, decomposition resumes, releasing carbon dioxide and increasing global warming. Indonesian forests are being destroyed by fires, logging, and farm building. All of these actions dry the soil and release carbon dioxide. Because the Congo basin peatland is remote and only recently discovered, it so far remains relatively undisturbed.

On Sumatra Island, some people dig channels through tropical peatland to drain the soil, which might increase the risk of fire.

A man plants a tree as part of the reforestation of a Tanzanian rain forest.

Chapter
FIVE

RESTORATION BY REFORESTATION

The best solution to deforestation is to develop management plans that allow sustainable use of forests and economic improvement of the region without destroying the forests. But many forests have already been clear-cut or burned so saving them is no longer an option. The next option is reforestation or restoration.

Ecological restoration is the process by which an ecosystem is recovered after it has been degraded, damaged, or destroyed. Restoration helps restore biodiversity and ecosystem health. It should be a component of all conservation and sustainable development programs. The FAO distinguishes between forest restoration and rehabilitation. In forest restoration, the goal is to return the forest to its original state, restoring both productivity and species diversity. In forest rehabilitation, the goal is restoring the original productivity and some, but not necessarily all, of the original species diversity. Both processes are meant to ensure that forests can again provide ecological services. They are intended to strengthen the forest so it can be used in the future. Reforestation simply means reestablishing any kind of forest on forest land that has been cleared. The return of forest to an area can be passive, meaning naturally occurring. It can also be active, with human intervention. Sometimes afforestation is used, when a forest is established in a region that was not previously forested.

REFORESTATION IN ASIA

Beginning in the 2000s, Vietnam's forest cover began to increase after decades of deforestation. Some natural forests were allowed to recover, and many trees were planted on previously unforested land. At the same time, agriculture was prospering, and Vietnam's exports of rice, coffee, rubber, and black pepper were increasing. Three policies contributed to Vietnam's forest improvements. First, the government changed from collective farming to individual farming and taught farmers modern techniques. Second, the Vietnamese government began giving local authorities more control over the forest, and third, in 2004, the government established the Payment for Forest Environmental Services (PFES) program.

The combination of small farms plus more control over surrounding forests encouraged farmers to conserve their own land. They decreased hillside cultivation and reforested. They grew crops on more fertile soils and added new crops, increasing productivity. Although much of the land in the PFES program belongs to the government, some of it enables small payments to farmers. These programs have all encouraged both reforestation and rural development. But although they decreased deforestation, they do not account for all of Vietnam's success. Approximately 40 percent of it is due to leakage—Vietnam decreased its own deforestation by importing timber cut in neighboring countries.[2] Thus, Vietnam is still only a partial success story.

German scientists are setting up bat roosting sites in deforested tropical areas. Bats fly long distances every night and eat fruits and nectar. They can speed up reforestation by rapidly dispersing seeds.

In India, more than 150 years of commercial use led to widespread forest degradation and deforestation. Since the late 1980s, India has been working to reverse deforestation and improve its forest cover. The government prioritized afforestation and reforestation. It also enrolled communities in forest management programs. The 1988 National Forest Policy decentralized forest management and made forestry less commercial. As of 2014, India has one of the world's largest community forest initiatives. Together, its 106,000 participating villages manage more than 54 million acres (22 million ha) of forest.[3]

REFORESTATION IN INDONESIA

Indonesia has the world's highest deforestation rate according to a 2014 study in the journal *Nature Climate Change*. Japanese businesses have taken an interest in reforesting of this area. Between 2005 and 2011, Mitsui Sumitomo Insurance undertook the Tropical Rainforest Recovery Project. It worked in an 865-acre (350 ha) area of the Paliyan Wildlife Reserve in Java. Cooperating with Indonesia's Department of Forestry, the company planted 300,000 native trees, fruit trees, and crops. By combining agriculture with forestry, it hoped to both restore the forest and improve the local economy. The agriculture would benefit the economy while the trees continued to grow. Project leaders expect the trees grown during the project will absorb 77,200 short tons (70,000 metric tons) of carbon dioxide in the 20 years after the project.[4]

Indonesia's 17,000 islands are home to 17 percent of the world's bird species, 12 percent of mammal species, and 16 percent of reptile and amphibian species.[6]

Daikin, a Japanese air-conditioning company, in cooperation with the NGO Conservation International, undertook a similar project, called the green wall, in Java's Gunung Gede Pangrango National Park. In 2008, the groups began planting trees on degraded land. They also helped the local population develop sustainable forms of income, including catfish ponds and ecotourism. In the process, locals are learning to both value and protect the forest. As of 2016, the green wall project had planted 120,000 trees on 740 acres (300 ha), and most were growing well.[5]

Gunung Gede Pangrango
National Park in Indonesia is also
a site for scientific research.

King vultures in El Salvador feed on dead animals, keeping the rain forests clean.

The Indonesian government is also working to protect its peatland forests. Following a series of destructive forest and peatland fires in 2015, it created the Peatland Restoration Agency. It hopes to designate all peatland areas in the country as protected areas.

FURTHER REFORESTATION EXAMPLES

In El Salvador, forests are coming back after being devastated by extremely high population density and a brutal civil war in the 1980s. During the war, hundreds of thousands of citizens left the country seeking safety. Following the 1992 Peace Accords, a democratic government formed and emigrants began to return. Forests also began to return. The 1992 Land Transfer Program distributed lands once held by massive agro-industries, giving them to one-fifth of rural households. This made land distribution much more equal. Economic development throughout the country also improved health and education. These factors linked strongly with the 16 percent increase in forests between 2001 and 2010.[7]

El Salvador's economy improved largely because of the contributions of emigrants returning after the war. They brought with them savings from their time abroad. This was especially important in rural areas. Areas with the greatest infusion of money showed the greatest improvement in forest regrowth. The recovering forest is still young and lacks a complete canopy. Much of it is coffee plantations shaded by native trees. Although not original forest, these areas are expanding biodiversity and increasing carbon storage. The high-quality coffee grown here is also improving the local economy. El Salvador is successfully restoring its forests.

Finally, the world's largest tropical forest restoration project is the Guanacaste Conservation Area (ACG) in Costa Rica. This dry tropical forest region was severely degraded by fires used to clear and maintain pasturelands. Native species, not adapted to fire, died out and were replaced by an invasive African grass, jaragua. The restoration program began in 1985, spearheaded by Dr. Daniel Janzen of the University of Pennsylvania

SAVING RAIN FORESTS WITH TREE CORRIDORS

Often, forests are broken into fragments by building roads, farms, or other features. But forests can continue to provide some ecosystem services if the fragmentation is done responsibly. One method is leaving tree corridors, or narrow bands of trees that connect remaining forest fragments. A Costa Rica study showed that, with corridors, pollinators could move among forest fragments and pollinate successfully. Isolated fragments had fewer pollinators, and many plants could not reproduce. The ability to move long distances is especially important for pollinators such as some hummingbirds.

Coffee shrubs need tall trees to provide shade. Coffee plantation owners in El Salvador can use native rain forest trees for this purpose.

and his wife, Dr. Winnie Hallwachs. The program bought up farmland and eliminated all fires within the ACG. Seedlings from adjoining areas were allowed to enter the areas naturally, carried by wind or animals. Native species began to return by natural succession. Natural, or ecological, succession happens when a region is left to change naturally without human intervention. Plants and animals enter the region from surrounding areas, and communities replace each other in sequence, gradually building the region's diversity and stability. The purchase of adjacent rain forest later expanded the ACG. It now contains 235,000 species of plants and animals.[8] Planting trees is something everyone can do, and it is one of the most important ways to restore the world's forests. It is essential in the tropics.

THE BILLION TREE CAMPAIGN

The UN Billion Tree Campaign asks people all over the world to plant one billion trees every year. The project was inspired by Nobel laureate Wangari Maathai, founder of Kenya's Green Belt Movement. The UN began the campaign in 2006 and transferred it in 2011 to the Plant for the Planet Foundation. The foundation strongly encourages planting native trees appropriate to the local environment. In its first five years, the program's website logged the planting of 12,585,293,312 trees.[9]

Preserving rain forests helps save delicate species of plants and animals.

Chapter SIX

CONSERVING BY PRESERVING

It is much easier to save a forest than restore it after it is gone. When rain forest land is set aside and protected from human uses, the ecosystem retains its health and function and continues to support its great biodiversity. Preservation may be done by governments, NGOs, private individuals, or any mixture of these. Protected land can have different levels of use. These include national parks or forests, indigenous lands, game preserves, and nature preserves. Considerable progress has been made. Between 1997 and 2003, tropical rain forest protection rose from 8.8 to 23.3 percent of the world's rain forest area, or nearly one-fourth.[1]

The Jane Goodall Institute works to protect chimpanzees in Gombe Stream National Park.

Another way to protect rain forests is to protect their animals, especially endangered species. Famous animal behaviorist Jane Goodall began her career in 1960 studying the chimpanzees of Gombe Stream National Park in Tanzania, Africa. By the 1970s, she was very concerned about changes to the rain forest. She watched as mining and logging destroyed the trees. She realized she must do something to help preserve the chimps' environment. In 1977, she founded a nonprofit organization, the Jane Goodall Institute, to promote conservation, education, and human rights. "I went to Africa as a scientist; I left the jungle as an activist," Goodall says.[2]

"There is still a window of time. Nature can win if we give her a chance."[4]

—Dr. Jane Goodall, scientist and conservationist

WORLD HERITAGE SITES

One goal of the UN is to protect irreplaceable sites that are part of the world's cultural and natural heritage—places as diverse as the Egyptian pyramids and Australia's Great Barrier Reef. These sites are designated by the United Nations Educational, Scientific and Cultural Organization (UNESCO) as World Heritage Sites. One World Heritage Site is the Central Amazon Conservation Complex, the largest protected area in the Amazon basin. Its nearly 15 million acres (6 million ha) include two national parks and two sustainable development reserves.[3] It is one of the most biodiverse regions on the planet.

Two Amazon rivers, the Negro and the Solimões, come together at this World Heritage Site, which contains examples of most of the Amazon's known ecosystems. These include dryland forests, periodically flooded lowland forests, rivers, waterfalls, swamps, lakes, and beaches. It is the habitat of several rare and endangered species, including the giant otter, Amazonian manatee, black caiman, and two freshwater dolphin species. The site contains 60 percent of the Amazon's fish species, 60 percent of its bird species, and a high diversity

THE AMAZON'S SWIMMING CAT

The jaguar is the largest cat in the Americas and a good swimmer. This beautiful, powerful cat has a large, rounded head, short legs, and a spotted coat. Its jaws and teeth are strong enough to bite through a turtle shell or a crocodile skull. Jaguars also eat other animals, including deer, monkeys, armadillos, and lizards. They roam over large areas, but, due to habitat destruction and threats from farmers and ranchers, their original range has shrunk by half. Jaguars are shy and seldom seen, so it is difficult to obtain exact counts, but their numbers are dropping.

of primates, especially monkeys.[5] It is also home to jaguars and harpy eagles.

THE PROTECTED AMAZON

Reducing deforestation is most successful where protected areas prevent any and all resources from being removed and where the rights and livelihoods of indigenous peoples are protected. These are the conclusions of a 2013 study of the Amazon rain forest by University of Michigan scientists. The researchers compared amounts of deforestation in three types of protected areas: strictly protected areas, sustainable-use areas, and indigenous lands.

Strictly protected areas included state and national biological stations, state and national parks, and biological reserves. They allow no removal of resources. Sustainable-use areas allow removal of resources such as trees, land use changes, and even human settlements. Many people thought strict protection areas would be controversial and unlikely to be implemented. But strict protection areas have been

Stopping deforestation also saves plants that are not trees, including bromeliads.

successful even where there are high deforestation pressures. Indigenous areas, where people depend on the forest for their lives, did especially well. These areas had the lowest deforestation rates.

More than half of the Brazilian Amazon—an area larger than Greenland—is now preserved in national parks or indigenous lands. These designations protect

"If we can keep healthy numbers of jaguar in the Amazon, we'll be closer to protecting the rainforest as a whole."[6]

—Jamie Gordon, regional manager for Brazil and Amazon Unit, WWF

the forest from both logging and agriculture. By protecting the rights of indigenous peoples, the Brazilian government ensured their cooperation in protecting the forest while also preserving the indigenous peoples' ways of life. Continued success of preservation programs, in the Amazon and elsewhere, depends on a combination of factors. Governments must have the will to preserve and maintain forests as well as enforce laws. Industries must cooperate, and international movements such as the UN REDD+ program, NGOs, and individuals must continue to exert pressure until rain forest protection becomes an accepted part of world culture.

SAVING AFRICAN RAIN FORESTS

Africa has preserved some of its unique and threatened rain forest in national parks and a few reserves. The six countries in the Congo basin came together in 1999 to form a system to track logging and poaching in the Congo. In 2000, they created Sangha Park, which protects more than 2.5 million acres (1 million ha) of rain forest in three countries.[7] As of 2017, the two largest protected regions in the Congo basin are the Dzanga-Sangha Complex of Protected Areas in the southwestern Central African Republic and the Moukalaba-Doudou National Park in Gabon.

Much of the West African rain forest has already been destroyed. The Upper Guinea Forests include Tai National Park, a UNESCO World Heritage Site in Ivory Coast. One-half of the plants and almost one-third of the animals in this 1,275-square-mile (3,302 sq km) park are endemic—they exist nowhere else on Earth. Nyungwe National Park in Rwanda and Kibira National Park in Burundi both protect parts of Rwanda's Nyungwe Forest, which contains almost 300 species of birds and a great diversity of primates.[8] Together, they form an important international reserve protecting African forests.

SAVING ENDANGERED SPECIES

One reason for establishing rain forest preserves is to protect their high biodiversity. And one way to protect biodiversity is to protect endangered species. Because saving the animal

The black-and-white colobus is one of the animals that lives in Tai National Park.

means saving its habitat as well, a good way to gain support for saving rain forests is to publicize their endangered species.

Rainforest Trust is one leader in this fight. In 2015, it announced the creation of seven reserves totaling 74,816 acres (30,277 ha) in Madagascar.[9] These new protected areas will stop loss of rain forests due to logging and mining. Rainforest Trust will also protect seven critically endangered species of lemurs, which are found only in Madagascar; the critically endangered golden mantella frog, which is endemic to the region; and other endemic species. GlobalGiving is a global crowdfunding community that connects nonprofits, donors, and companies around the world to put together important projects. One of its projects is the Bonobo Conservation Initiative (BCI). Bonobos, which live in the rain forests of the Democratic Republic of the Congo (DRC), are endangered by bushmeat hunting and habitat

Several lemur species are critically endangered, including the red ruffed lemur.

MOUNTAIN GORILLA: AFRICAN RAIN FOREST'S ICONIC SPECIES

Loss of rain forest means loss of many iconic animals. The critically endangered mountain gorilla lives in three countries in eastern and central Africa. An estimated 575 to 640 mountain gorillas still exist.[13] All live in the wild. Mountain gorillas are gentle, playful, highly intelligent animals. They live together in groups and are vegetarians. They use tools and communicate with each other. The most significant threat to mountain gorillas is habitat loss due to deforestation and forest degradation. Other threats are human diseases and poaching. Because they lack immunity to human diseases and their populations are already small, they may be easily wiped out by a disease that is relatively harmless to humans. The most serious poaching threat is accidental death by snares set up to catch antelope, bush pigs, and other game.

destruction. BCI will fund salaries, equipment, and supplies for 112 locals who work as eco-guards.[10] These eco-guards protect the bonobos and track the populations. There are many more initiatives such as these.

Poaching, or illegal hunting, may threaten the success of many preserves. In 2015, a team of scientists surveyed a region deep inside the Dja Faunal Reserve in Cameroon, Africa. This World Heritage Site covers 1.3 million acres (526,000 ha) of the Congo basin. The team looked for signs of the 50-plus mammal species that live in the reserve, such as chimps and western lowland gorillas. Team members eventually found a few traces of 36 species. But they also found 16 hunting camps and massive numbers of gun cartridges.[11] By 2017, they had covered only a small portion of the reserve and still hoped to find more animals in the region's remote swamplands.

The Dja Reserve is typical of the situation in central African rain forests. Elephants are being killed for their ivory and are declining by 9 percent per year.[12] Demand for bushmeat, including chimpanzees, gorillas, forest antelopes, and bush pigs, is growing in large cities, increasing illegal hunting. Bushmeat costs more than domestically produced meats, but it is considered a status symbol. Approximately half of the illegal bushmeat is sold; the other half is eaten by villagers near reserves.

Governments, NGOs, and other donor organizations concerned about the threat of poaching have identified two ways to tackle it. The first is better enforcement of hunting laws. New tracking devices attached to animals transmit GPS information to anti-poaching teams, making enforcement much more efficient. The second, longer-term goal is changing the culture of communities surrounding the Dja Faunal Reserve. This involves creating livelihoods for natives that do not involve poaching, as well as developing an understanding of the value of wildlife so people will want to protect rather than hunt it.

SAVING PANGOLINS

Pangolins, or scaly anteaters, are the world's most trafficked mammals. All eight species of pangolins are on the IUCN's Red List of endangered species; some are critically endangered. Pangolins are illegally hunted and trafficked for their meat and scales. Pangolin meat is considered a status symbol in some Asian countries, and their scales are used in Chinese medicine. Many countries have banned pangolin hunting and trafficking, but the IUCN estimates more than one million were killed between 2004 and 2014.[14] The key to saving pangolins is stopping their removal from the wild. This requires learning more about pangolins' life history, training rangers to find where pangolins are being hunted, and providing rangers with resources to stop poachers. It also involves increasing locals' awareness of the problem and of the benefits of pangolin conservation.

TROPICAL DRY FORESTS

The phrase *tropical forest* usually conjures thoughts of a teeming jungle that is always warm and wet. In a rain forest, this is true. But not all tropical forests receive rain all year round. For several months every year, dry tropical forests receive little or no rainfall, followed by a very wet season. Similarly to rain forests, dry tropical forests are warm all year, but they receive only 10 to 80 inches (25 to 200 cm) of rain per year.[15]

Dry forests occur in tropical and subtropical regions. These include eastern Bolivia and central Brazil, the coasts of Ecuador and Peru, the Caribbean, central India, Madagascar, southern Mexico, valleys of the northern Andes, and southeastern Africa. Plants in these regions must adapt to dry seasons. Most trees are deciduous. During the dry season, when they lose their leaves and the canopy opens up, sunlight reaches the ground. Thus, understory growth is much thicker than in rain forests. Dry tropical forests are less biodiverse than rain forests, but much more diverse than temperate forests. A 0.25 acre (0.1 ha) plot has between 50 and 70 species of trees and large shrubs.[16]

Monkeys, large cats, parrots, rodents, amphibians, and reptiles roam through dry tropical forests. Amphibians, which must maintain moist skin, often hibernate during the summer dry season, a behavior known as estivation. Dry forests can have 200 to 300 species of birds.[17]

Dry tropical forests are more endangered than rain forests because they are easily converted into agricultural land. Many animals face extinction due to loss of habitat. Owing largely to the efforts of Dr. Daniel Janzen, much of Costa Rica's dry forest has been restored as the Guanacaste Conservation Area.

Tropical dry forests have deciduous trees—trees that lose their leaves during the dry season.

Rain forest ecotourism provides locals with jobs such as being a tour guide, and it also educates others about the importance of an ecosystem.

Chapter SEVEN

OUTSIDE HELP AND COOPERATION

Tropical forests are appreciated by people around the world. People recognize their beauty and their vital role in safeguarding world climate and biodiversity. Thus, help and protection often comes from outside the forests. NGOs are one source of outside help. These citizen activists tirelessly advocate for rain forests, doing everything from fund-raising to taking political action to planting trees. Another source is ecotourism, which enables tourists to visit rain forests. Ecotourism

RAIN FOREST NGOS

Some well-known and active environmental NGOs are working to save tropical forests. These include Environmental Defense Fund, Friends of the Earth, Global Forest Watch, Greenpeace, IUCN, the Nature Conservancy, Rainforest Alliance, RAN, Rainforest Foundation US, Rainforest Rescue, Rainforest Trust, Sierra Club, and WWF.

is a win-win situation. Local people receive economic benefits from tourists, improving their lives while preserving their forests. Tourists get to experience the rain forest firsthand.

NGOS AND WHAT THEY DO

NGOs may be local, national, or international in scope. They are created to act on a specific type of issue, often social or environmental. According to the World Bank, the two general types of NGOs are operational NGOs, which conduct development projects, and advocacy NGOs, which promote specific causes. Some NGOs do both. Citizens can become members of some NGOs by paying an annual membership fee.

Depending on size and funds available, NGOs may rely on volunteers, paid staff, or both. NGOs cannot make a profit, but they need funding to carry out their goals. The funding comes from membership dues, grants, private donations, and sale of goods and services. Some even rely on government funding. Many environmental NGOs form because private citizens become frustrated at the failure of governments to act on environmental problems they think are critical.

Governments may fail to act because of a lack of political will, conflicts between political and economic priorities, disbelief in or ignorance of the science, or a decision that the costs of action are greater than the benefits. When problems are international, such as rain forest destruction, action becomes even harder. International treaties can be weak and difficult to enforce, and there is no global authority to coordinate efforts. NGOs step into these situations. They do research, lobby governments and monitor their actions, keep pressure on industries, and inform the public. Perhaps their most important function is to build coalitions of governments and other NGOs to make sure action is taken.

> "Activist groups . . . are watchdogs of projects that impact the rainforest, and they spread the word to other organizations, peoples, and governments."[2]
>
> —Rhett Butler, founder of Mongabay and cofounder of journal Tropical Conservation Science, 2012

One organization dedicated to rain forest protection is RAN. RAN has three goals: to preserve rain forests, protect the climate, and uphold human rights. The group chooses campaigns strategically, where they will do the most good, and frequently develops partnerships with other groups. RAN's first campaign, in 1985, pressured Burger King to cancel $35 million in contracts to buy Central American beef.[1] This successful campaign stopped rain forest land from being converted into cattle grazing land. RAN also provides community grants to other NGOs and to communities in Indonesia affected by deforestation by the pulp and paper industry.

Some NGOs working for rain forest protection are general organizations, with projects in many environmental areas. These include Greenpeace and the WWF. The WWF is one member of the Congo Basin Forest Partnership, which forms agreements between governments, enabling park and patrol staff to work across borders to stop poaching. The WWF helps local communities protect the forests and improve their economic status. It is also part of a tree plantation project in the DRC. It has planted 10 million trees to help local people and to protect mountain gorilla habitat.[3] The WWF is also working to provide fuel-efficient stoves and to help people find alternative wood sources to protect remaining forests.

NGOs such as RAN, the WWF, and many others all welcome individual memberships. Anyone can become a member with a yearly donation. They also have programs allowing interested people to adopt, or sponsor, endangered rain forest animals, such as gorillas or elephants. Funds go to projects that protect these animals. This is the easiest way to help

The WWF monitors logging operations in countries such as Gabon to make sure trees are taken sustainably and legally.

HOW INDIVIDUALS CAN SAVE RAIN FORESTS

General ways to save rain forests are summarized using the abbreviation TREES:

- **T**each others about rain forests.
- **R**estore forests by planting trees.
- **E**ncourage lifestyles that do not damage rain forests.
- **E**stablish protected rain forest parks.
- **S**upport companies that run sustainably.

Everyday actions based on these guidelines include supporting businesses that sell sustainably produced products and pressuring those that do not. People should not buy pets that might be imported illegally, such as parrots or iguanas. Other actions include cutting down on the use of wood and paper products such as paper plates and using products with a high recycled content. People can also reduce their consumption of fast-food hamburgers to decrease demand for cattle pastures in rain forest areas. Fast food often contains rain forest beef, but this beef is not labeled when it enters the United States. Because its source cannot be traced, the only way to reduce the demand for rain forest beef is to reduce consumption of sources known to contain it.

support rain forest projects. Most also seek volunteers for specific projects described on their websites.

RAIN FOREST ECOTOURISM

Ecotourism saves rain forests by jump-starting the local economy. Ecotourists pay to see the rain forest unspoiled, giving local people an incentive to preserve it. Money spent by tourists for entrance fees, tours, food, housing, or local crafts goes directly into the local economy. Ecotourism provides jobs for locals as guides, park rangers, and hotel workers. People who have good jobs no longer need to poach wildlife to make a living. Ecotourism even benefits local education. NGOs and other groups supporting ecotourism provide training for tour guides and park rangers. Some conservation groups donate directly to local schools.

However, ecotourism must be handled sustainably. If it grows too fast, it may result in a mass-market approach, which can damage both the environment and the local economy. It may result in hotels being

Ecotourism can provide locals with a wider customer base of people who will buy jewelry or souvenirs.

VOLUNTEER ECOTOURISTS

Some ecotourists do more than only tour—they work. Organizations such as GoEco give people the opportunity to do volunteer conservation work in far-flung locations. Volunteers might work at a wildlife sanctuary in South Africa or do conservation and research with animals. These might include orangutans in Malaysia, a variety of wildlife in Madagascar, or tapirs in Costa Rica, pictured. They might participate in a rain forest expedition in Costa Rica or care for orphaned chimpanzees in Zambia. Volunteers can choose from most continents and many projects. Project times range from one to 12 weeks.

built in environmentally fragile areas or resources such as trees being destroyed. For example, some Costa Rican parks now have far too many tourists, and orangutans in some Indonesian forests are dying due to diseases caught from tourists. Careful planning and management, combined with adequate facilities, are needed to maintain sustainable ecotourism.

Ecotourist opportunities are available in most rain forest areas, including the Amazon, Central America, Madagascar, and Central and East Africa. Most ecotourists take tours or safaris offered by tourism companies. For example, one travel company offers a tour tracking gorillas and chimpanzees in Uganda's Bwindi Impenetrable Forest, a highly biodiverse UNESCO World Heritage Site. The same tour visits Kibale Forest to observe other primate species in the wild and Queen Elizabeth National Park to see lions, leopards, elephants, and other wildlife.

In the Amazon, many people travel to Manaus, Brazil, where they embark on trips into the rain forest or cruises up the Amazon River. Peru's Manu Biosphere

Reserve, a UNESCO World Heritage Site, is especially prized by bird-watchers because of its thousands of types of exotic birds, many of which are nearly extinct elsewhere in the Amazon. Bolivia's Madidi National Park offers jungle hikes as well as animal watching and bird-watching. Some indigenous groups allow tourists to participate in their communities by helping build houses or boats or making bows, arrows, or baskets. This ecotourism benefits the local economy and increases the tourists' awareness and understanding of indigenous peoples.

Both NGOs and ecotourism represent ways in which everyone can contribute to saving the world's rain forests. An individual's contribution can range from an annual membership in an NGO to a long-term volunteer vacation to do hands-on work planting trees, caring for wildlife, or doing environmental research. Every contribution helps the rain forest.

INDIGENOUS PEOPLES AND ECOTOURISM

Posada Amazonas is an ecotourist lodge located in the Madre de Dios region of Peru, jointly owned by a community of indigenous Ese'Eja and Rainforest Expeditions, a tourism company in Peru. This joint project has resulted in higher incomes and better social services for the Ese'Eja, especially compared to the results of other land uses, such as logging. It has also protected the area's endangered wildlife. The Ese'Eja are changing their attitudes toward wildlife. They are less inclined to hunt endangered species such as giant otters and harpy eagles. One section of the land owned by the Ese'Eja includes a small ethnobotanic center. There, a local *eyámikekwa*, similar to a shaman, shares his vast knowledge of the region's medicinal plants.

"Ecotourism has the best chance of being a boon to indigenous peoples where they have control over their lands, and tourist developments are in accord with their own visions of their future."[4]

—*Cultural Survival Inc., an organization that supports indigenous peoples around the world, 1999*

Preserving the rain forests that still exist is the first step in sustainable forest management.

EIGHT

THE FUTURE OF TROPICAL FORESTS

I n a 2014 collection titled *Deforestation Success Stories*, the Union of Concerned Scientists describes how various tropical countries have slowed their rates of deforestation and started on the path to sustainable forest management. All countries go through a process known as forest transition. That is, they first increase and then decrease their deforestation rates, finally transitioning to reforestation. Countries in all three stages are working on forest management. These include

Insects may be hard to spot in rain forests, but they are also harmed by deforestation.

high-forest, low-deforestation countries such as Guyana and several central African nations such as Gabon and Cameroon. These also include countries with high deforestation rates, such as Brazil, Tanzania, and Madagascar; and countries already reforesting, such as Costa Rica, El Salvador, India, and Vietnam. Future successes for most countries will involve some combination of these tactics.

"In order for the forest to be preserved, the underlying social, economic, and political reasons for deforestation must be recognized and addressed."[1]

—Rhett Butler, founder of Mongabay and cofounder of journal Tropical Conservation Science, 2012

A POSSIBLE FUTURE

S. Joseph Wright of the Smithsonian Tropical Research Institute summarizes five anthropogenic, or human-caused, factors driving the future of forests: land-use change such as deforestation or reforestation; wood extraction such as by logging or harvesting fuelwood; hunting, especially by poaching; atmospheric change, including increasing greenhouse gas levels; and climate change, including increasing temperatures, changes in precipitation, and stronger storms. Wright notes that giving forests protected status can affect the first two factors, but poaching often continues despite a forest's protected status. And of course, this status offers no protection from atmospheric and climate changes.

SUSTAINABLE TROPICAL WOOD PRODUCTS

The growing demand for wood products is helping destroy tropical forests. The Union of Concerned Scientists wants to satisfy the demand for wood without destroying the forests. The group's report, *Planting for the Future*, suggests using a combination of new management practices, effective policy, and enlightened consumers. One technique is timber tracking, a process for tracking timber from its source to the consumer. This enables consumers to know where their wood comes from. Another is multispecies plantations, which grow several species on the same plot, rather than monocultures. Studies have shown that multispecies plantations improve soil, growth rates, and timber yields when compared to monocultures. Diseases and pests also do less damage to these plantations. Increased consumer demand for goods such as sustainable wood can encourage companies to use sustainable practices.

Temperate forests have already gone through many of the worst effects of these anthropogenic factors, but Wright thinks three characteristics of tropical forests may make the transition easier. First, it is much more difficult to convert tropical forests to agricultural use, which may help protect them. Second, even if converted, new agricultural land may be quickly abandoned, and abandoned land regenerates rapidly. Within a few decades, the new

The boundaries between primary and secondary rain forest can be apparent with an aerial view. Secondary-forest trees are much shorter when young.

growth can produce a forest structure that supports much wildlife. Third, an impressive network of protected rain forest already exists. These areas can cushion the effect of continuing exploitation.

Leaving aside coming changes to atmosphere and climate, Wright sees several future trends in rain forests. First, continuing conversion to agriculture will cause large net losses in rain forest land, particularly in South America and Southeast Asia. This will be somewhat offset as abandoned land is reforested. However, reforestation produces young secondary forest, not mature rain forest. Trees are smaller, storing less carbon. The canopy is more open, leading to less diversity in species living there. Logging is increasing in Africa, Indonesia, and South America, and cutting for fuelwood is also increasing in many areas. Most effects are near inhabited areas, but tree cutting is increasingly reaching forest interiors. Hunters, too, reach deep into forests and remove valuable species. However, despite continued exploitation, extreme levels of rain forest loss are unlikely. Models project that between 64 and 89 percent of the forest cover in the 2000s will still exist in 2050, although it will be depleted of many valuable trees, game species, and fuelwood.[2]

HUMAN POPULATION VERSUS BIODIVERSITY

Scott Mori, a scientist at the New York Botanical Garden, has watched the decline of rain forest biodiversity and fears for the future. Tropical soils, he points out, cannot support high human populations without adding excessive fertilizers and pesticides. "If tropical areas are not productive enough today to provide significant resources to a world population of 6.5 billion," he asked in 2013, "what makes humans think that they will be able to contribute to supporting a population of nine to 11 billion humans by 2050?"[3] He understated the world's population; in 2013, it was more than 7.1 billion.[4] By 2017, it had grown to more than 7.5 billion.[5] Mori says that protecting rain forest biodiversity would require controlling both human population growth and per capita consumption. Among other things, this would lead to higher prices for rain forest products.

But the world's changing climate is already affecting rain forests. This is evident in the amount of biomass, the types of tree species present, and the rates at which new trees replace old trees. The changes are occurring in remote and protected forests, suggesting they are due to climate and atmospheric change, not direct human exploitation. But no one yet knows specifically how the changes are happening or what forest mechanisms are different now. There is also no agreement on how these changes will eventually affect the forest. Scientists only know the forest is evolving.

ADAPTING TO FUTURE FOREST CHANGES

Tropical forest journalist Rhett Butler thinks the past approach of establishing parks and other protected areas is not sufficient to protect forests in the future. Parks provide too little economic benefit to poor

Boardwalks in rain forest parks allow visitors to enjoy the forests while protecting the ecosystem from damage.

CHANGING INDUSTRY LEADERS

The palm oil corporation Wilmar buys palm oil, pictured, from 80 percent of the world's suppliers.[6] If it pledged to buy only from companies committed to not cutting rain forest, other companies would follow, resulting in both lower deforestation and lower carbon dioxide emissions. For a year, Wilmar's CEO, Kuok Khoon Hong, worked with Glenn Hurowitz, founder of Forest Heroes. Hurowitz showed Kuok the protests occurring at his client companies, such as Kellogg's. Kuok worked even more closely with Scott Poynton of the Forest Trust, which teaches companies how to stop deforestation. On December 5, 2013, Kuok signed a pledge to buy only from companies not cutting rain forest. Within another year, nearly all palm oil traders had signed similar pledges.

local inhabitants, who depend on forest resources for their livelihoods. Butler advocates new agricultural techniques and enhanced economic opportunities for inhabitants in and around tropical forests. Such techniques will benefit both people and forests. Although it will be difficult, he emphasizes the need for tropical agriculture and industry to adopt sustainable methods. In already deforested areas, he advocates management to increase productivity and sustainability of the new ecosystems: farms, pastures, plantations, and scrubland. Improving these lands will decrease the need to clear more forests. In areas with some remaining forest, active reforestation will speed the recovery of the forest.

Many scientists and conservationists have long recognized that climate change is the major challenge of the coming decades. Climate change increases as more greenhouse gases enter the atmosphere. Saving rain forests may be the best solution to this crisis, as trees pull carbon dioxide out of the atmosphere and store it in their wood and the forest soil. More and bigger trees mean more carbon storage, which in turn means less climate change. This is especially true for tropical trees, some of which remove carbon dioxide all year round with no winter dormant period.

Forest destruction has released much of the excess carbon that is helping warm the planet. But in the 2000s, growing environmental movements and pressure from citizens are beginning to have an effect. Governments and industries are becoming serious about developing and maintaining sustainable practices. This means slowing deforestation and encouraging reforestation on a massive scale. If the current trend continues, this would save the forests and their biodiversity while also locking up much of the excess carbon for as long as the trees exist. "The public should take heart," says Rolf Skar of Greenpeace. "We are at a potentially historic moment where the world is starting to wake up to this issue, and to apply real solutions."[7]

> "Every time I hear about a government program that is going to spend billions of dollars on some carbon capture and storage program, I just laugh and think, what is wrong with a tree?"[8]
>
> —Nigel Sizer, director of forest programs, World Resources Institute, 2014

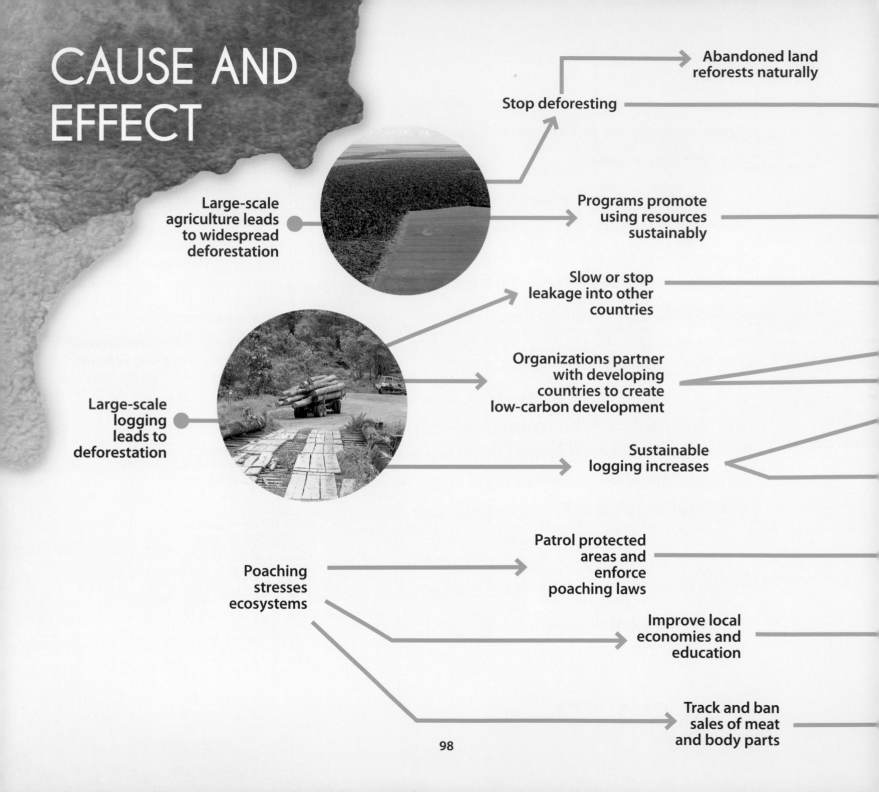

CAUSE AND EFFECT

Large-scale agriculture leads to widespread deforestation

Stop deforesting

Abandoned land reforests naturally

Programs promote using resources sustainably

Slow or stop leakage into other countries

Large-scale logging leads to deforestation

Organizations partner with developing countries to create low-carbon development

Sustainable logging increases

Poaching stresses ecosystems

Patrol protected areas and enforce poaching laws

Improve local economies and education

Track and ban sales of meat and body parts

98

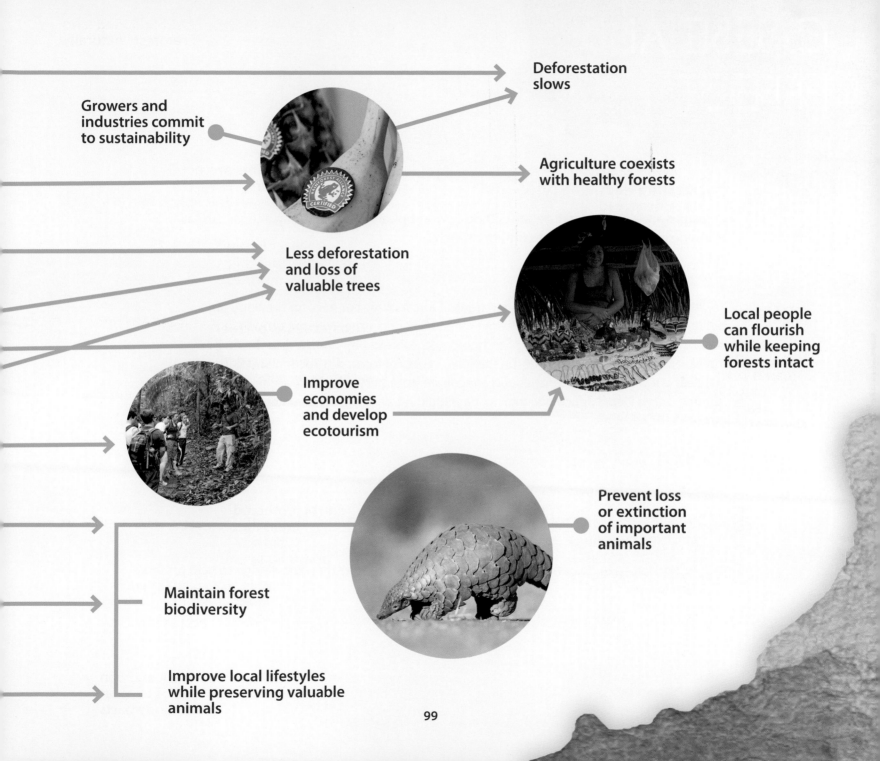

Deforestation slows

Growers and industries commit to sustainability

Agriculture coexists with healthy forests

Less deforestation and loss of valuable trees

Local people can flourish while keeping forests intact

Improve economies and develop ecotourism

Prevent loss or extinction of important animals

Maintain forest biodiversity

Improve local lifestyles while preserving valuable animals

99

ESSENTIAL
FACTS

WHAT IS HAPPENING

Industries and some individuals are cutting down tropical forests, reducing animal habitat and releasing greenhouse gases into the atmosphere.

THE CAUSES

For thousands of years, people living in tropical forests have cut trees for firewood and building materials, and they have cleared forests for agriculture. With the growth of the human population and the development of technology, these and other dangers to the forests have increased exponentially. In the 2010s, the main causes of forest destruction and degradation are clear-cutting for cattle ranches and agriculture, commercial logging, logging for fuelwood, hunting (often illegal poaching), mining, dam building, and climatic changes due to increased atmospheric carbon.

KEY PLAYERS

- Governments, organizations, and industries adopt regulations to preserve the rain forests.

- Scientists research what is happening and advise organizations and governments on how to solve the problem.

- Indigenous peoples who live in and around rain forests use their knowledge to help preserve rain forests.

- Politicians create laws and policies that protect and restore tropical forests.

WHAT IS BEING DONE TO FIX THE DAMAGE

The first goal is to stop, or at least slow, deforestation. For already-deforested areas, reforestation is necessary. This is sometimes as simple as letting abandoned forest regenerate. But people may also assist the process with the goal of restoration, or returning the forest to its original state. Both reforestation and stopping deforestation are most successful when local and indigenous communities are empowered to control forest management.

WHAT IT MEANS FOR THE FUTURE

Saving rain forests requires persistence to carry out, on a larger scale, the necessary changes. But the most significant challenge in the future will be controlling the rise of greenhouse gases and the rate of climate change, which is caused by an excess of those gases. Saving rain forests is one part of this. Rain forest carbon storage lowers atmospheric greenhouse gases and decreases global temperatures. But much of the work of saving rain forests must be done outside the rain forest by controlling the use of fossil fuels in the energy and transportation sectors.

QUOTE

"Destroying rain forest for economic gain . . . is like burning a Renaissance painting to cook a meal."

—Biologist E. O. Wilson, 1990

GLOSSARY

BIODIVERSITY

The variety of life in a particular habitat or ecosystem.

BIOMASS

An amount of living things in an area.

BUSHMEAT

Meat that comes from animals hunted in Asia or Africa.

CARBON SINK

A part of the natural environment, such as a forest or ocean, capable of absorbing and storing carbon.

DEFORESTATION

Permanent removal of a forest or stand of trees and conversion of the land to another use.

DETRITUS

Debris from disintegrated things.

ECOTOURISM

Visiting a habitat while avoiding activities that might damage it.

FERAL

Relating to a domestic animal that has escaped captivity and become wild or the offspring of such.

FRAGMENTATION

Cutting portions of habitats while leaving other portions, or fragments, intact as small isolated patches.

GREENHOUSE GAS

A gas that absorbs infrared radiation and traps heat in the atmosphere.

INDIGENOUS

Originating in or native to a place.

MONOCULTURE

The growing of a single crop or animal.

MORATORIUM

A temporary ban or prohibition of an activity such as logging.

NONGOVERNMENTAL ORGANIZATION

An independent organization not controlled by governments and often funded by donations and run by volunteers, abbreviated as NGO.

NONPROFIT

An organization that is not run to make a profit.

POACH

To illegally hunt or catch animals or fish.

REFORESTATION

Reestablishing any kind of forest (native, exotic, or monoculture) on land that has been cleared.

RESILIENCE

The ability of an ecosystem or living thing to respond to a disturbance by resisting damage and recovering quickly.

SUBSISTENCE FARMING

Farming that provides most of what the farmer needs to live and work but not much to sell.

SWIDDEN AGRICULTURE

A farming method that prepares crop fields by cutting and burning forests or woodlands.

VIRGIN FOREST

An area with old, mature trees that have not been disturbed significantly by people.

ADDITIONAL RESOURCES

SELECTED BIBLIOGRAPHY

Boucher, Doug, et al. "Deforestation Success Stories." *Union of Concerned Scientists*. Union of Concerned Scientists, June 2014. Web. 12 July 2017.

Butler, Rhett. "How to Save Tropical Rainforests." *Mongabay*. Mongabay. 22 July 2012. Web. 12 July 2017.

Fleshman, Michael. "Saving Africa's Forests, the 'Lungs of the World.'" *Africa Renewal*. Africa Renewal, Jan. 2008. Web. 12 July 2017.

Malhi, Yadvinder, et al. "African Rainforests: Past, Present, and Future." *Philosophical Transactions of the Royal Society: Biological Sciences* 368.1625 (5 Sept. 2013). *The Royal Society*. Web. 12 July 2017.

FURTHER READINGS

Blackwell, Lewis. *Rainforest*. New York: Abrams, 2014. Print.

Henningfeld, Diane Andrews. *Nature and Wildlife*. Detroit, MI: Greenhaven, 2011. Print.

Montgomery, Sy. *Amazon Adventure: How Tiny Fish Are Saving the World's Largest Rainforest*. Boston, MA: Houghton Mifflin, 2017. Print.

ONLINE RESOURCES

Booklinks
NONFICTION NETWORK
FREE! ONLINE NONFICTION RESOURCES

To learn more about tropical forest conservation, visit **abdobooklinks.com**. These links are routinely monitored and updated to provide the most current information available.

MORE INFORMATION

For more information on this subject, contact or visit the following organizations:

Amazon Conservation Team (ACT)

4211 N. Fairfax Drive
Arlington, VA 22203
703-522-4684
amazonteam.org

The ACT is a nonprofit organization that partners with indigenous groups in the Amazon to protect the rain forest.

Rainforest Action Network (RAN)

425 Bush Street, Suite 300
San Francisco, CA 94108
415-398-4404
ran.org

RAN protects human rights, the climate, and rain forests, and it fights strongly against deforestation.

SOURCE NOTES

CHAPTER 1. BRAZIL: A RAIN FOREST SUCCESS STORY

1. Doug Boucher, et al. "Deforestation Success Stories." *Union of Concerned Scientists*. Union of Concerned Scientists, 2014. Web. 19 Sept. 2017.

2. Brad Plumer. "Brazil's Recent Fight Against Deforestation Has Been a Huge Success." *Vox*. Vox Media, 14 June 2014. Web. 19 Sept. 2017.

3. Doug Boucher, et al. "Deforestation Success Stories." *Union of Concerned Scientists*. Union of Concerned Scientists, 2014. Web. 19 Sept. 2017.

4. Rhett Butler. "Amazon Destruction." *Mongabay*. Mongabay, 26 Jan. 2017. Web. 19 Sept. 2017.

5. "Amazon Rainforest Tribe Facts." *Tropical Rainforest Facts*. Tropical Rainforest Facts, n.d. Web. 19 Sept. 2017.

6. Scott Wallace. "Rare Photos of Brazilian Tribe Spur Pleas to Protect It." *National Geographic*. National Geographic Partners, 22 Nov. 2016. Web. 19 Sept. 2017.

7. Cristina Ramirez. "Akuntsu: Indigenous People of the Amazon." *Amazon Aid*. Amazon Aid, 21 July 2014. Web. 19 Sept. 2017.

8. "Amazon Rain Forest." *Mongabay*. Mongabay, n.d. Web. 19 Sept. 2017.

9. Lulu Garcia-Navarro. "Deep in the Amazon, an Unseen Battle over the Most Valuable Trees." *NPR*. NPR, 4 Nov. 2015. Web. 19 Sept. 2017.

10. "Where Are the Rainforests?" *Caltech*. California Institute of Technology, n.d. Web. 19 Sept. 2017.

11. "Tropical Rainforests." *Blue Planet Biomes*. Blue Planet Biomes, n.d. Web. 14 May 2017.

12. Ibid.

13. "Buttress Roots." *Caltech*. California Institute of Technology, n.d. Web. 19 Sept. 2017.

14. "Questions and Answers about Biodiversity." *Rainforest Rescue*. Rainforest Rescue, n.d. Web. 19 Sept. 2017.

15. Michael Evans. "Rainforests." *Earth Times*. Earth Times, 27 Apr. 2011. Web. 19 Sept. 2017.

16. Eva Botkin-Kowacki. "Deforestation: Brazil Is a Success Story for Conservation." *Christian Science Monitor*. Christian Science Monitor, 28 Apr. 2014. Web. 19 Sept. 2017.

17. Suzanne Goldenberg, et al. "Brazil Announces Massive Reforestation and Renewable Energy Plan with US." *Guardian*. Guardian, 30 June 2015. Web. 19 Sept. 2017.

18. Doug Boucher, et al. "Deforestation Success Stories." *Union of Concerned Scientists*. Union of Concerned Scientists, 2014. Web. 19 Sept. 2017.

19. "Protecting the Amazon for Life." *WWF*. WWF, 21 May 2014. Web. 19 Sept. 2017.

CHAPTER 2. THE VALUE AND THE THREAT

1. "Tropical Forests the Size of India 'Set to Be Lost by 2050.'" *Straits Times*. Singapore Press Holdings, 26 Aug. 2015. Web. 19 Sept. 2017.

2. Morgan Kelly. "If a Tree Falls in Brazil . . . ? Amazon Deforestation Could Mean Droughts for Western US." *Princeton University*. Princeton University, 7 Nov. 2013. Web. 19 Sept. 2017.

3. "Why Are Rainforests Important?" *Rainforest Concern*. Rainforest Concern, 2008. Web. 19 Sept. 2017.

4. "Rainforests: Why Are They Important?" *YPTE*. Young People's Trust for the Environment, 2017. Web. 19 Sept. 2017.

5. "The Disappearing Rainforests." *Raintree*. Raintree, 21 Dec. 2012. Web. 19 Sept. 2017.

6. Gary Braasch. "The Secret Life of a Tree in a Rain Forest." *Gary Braasch Environmental Photography*. Gary Braasch Environmental Photography, n.d. Web. 19 Sept. 2017.

7. "Why Are Rainforests Important?" *Rainforest Concern*. Rainforest Concern, 2008. Web. 19 Sept. 2017.

8. "The Disappearing Rainforests." *Raintree*. Raintree, 21 Dec. 2012. Web. 19 Sept. 2017.

9. "What Are Rainforests?" *Earth Eclipse*. Earth Eclipse, 2017. Web. 19 Sept. 2017.

10. Ryszard Laskowski. "Threats to Tropical Forests and What We Can Do About It." *Institute of Environmental Sciences*, Jagiellonian University, n.d. Web. 19 Sept. 2017.

11. John Vidal. "We Are Destroying Rainforests So Quickly They May Be Gone in 100 Years." *Guardian*. Guardian, 23 Jan. 2017. Web. 19 Sept. 2017.

12. "What Are Rainforests?" *Earth Eclipse*. Earth Eclipse, 2017. Web. 19 Sept. 2017.

13. "Unsustainable Cattle Ranching." *WWF*. WWF, 2017. Web. 19 Sept. 2017.

14. "What Are Rainforests?" *Earth Eclipse*. Earth Eclipse, 2017. Web. 19 Sept. 2017.

15. "Edward O. Wilson." *Today in Science History*. Today in Science History, 2017. Web. 19 Sept. 2017.

16. Gethin Chamberlain. "'They're Killing Us': World's Most Endangered Tribe Cries for Help." *Guardian*. Guardian, 21 Apr. 2012. Web. 19 Sept. 2017.

17. Leslie Taylor. *The Healing Power of Rainforest Herbs*. Garden City, NY: Square One Publishers, 2004. *Raintree*. Web. 19 Sept. 2017.

18. "Indonesia's Rainforests: Biodiversity and Endangered Species." *Rainforest Action Network*. RAN, n.d. Web. May 23, 2017.

19. "Tropical Rainforests." *Blue Planet Biomes*. Blue Planet Biomes, n.d. Web. 14 May 2017.

20. Ibid.

21. Ibid.

22. "Tropical Rainforest Layers." *Missouri Botanical Garden*. Missouri Botanical Garden, 2002. Web. 19 Sept. 2017.

23. "Tropical Rainforest Layers." *Missouri Botanical Garden*. Missouri Botanical Garden, 2002. Web. 19 Sept. 2017.

CHAPTER 3. SAVING FORESTS BY SAVING PEOPLE

1. Joe DeCapua. "African Rainforests Continue to Face Challenges." *VOA*. VOA, 5 Jan. 2012. Web. 19 Sept. 2017.

2. Rhett Butler. "How to Save Tropical Rainforests." *Mongabay*. Mongabay, 22 July 2017. Web. 19 Sept. 2017.

3. "Central America." *Passport to Knowledge*. Passport to Knowledge, 2005. Web. 19 Sept. 2017.

4. "How Chocolate Is Saving the Rainforest." *Cool Earth*. Cool Earth, 23 Mar. 2016. Web. 19 Sept. 2017.

5. Doug Boucher, et al. "Deforestation Success Stories." *Union of Concerned Scientists*. Union of Concerned Scientists, 2014. Web. 19 Sept. 2017.

6. Ibid. 21–23.

7. "Carnegie Science: The Newsletter of the Carnegie Institution, Fall 2007." Washington, DC: Carnegie Institution of Washington, 2007. *Carnegie Science*. Web. 19 Sept. 2017.

8. Doug Boucher, et al. "Deforestation Success Stories." *Union of Concerned Scientists*. Union of Concerned Scientists, 2014. Web. 19 Sept. 2017.

9. Sandra Cuffe. "Community Rights: A Key to Conservation in Central America." *Mongabay*. Mongabay, 9 Dec. 2016. Web. 19 Sept. 2017.

10. Ibid.

CHAPTER 4. SLOWING OR STOPPING DEFORESTATION

1. Mike Gaworecki. "New Study Analyzes Biggest Threats to Southeast Asian Biodiversity." *Mongabay*. Mongabay, 12 Jan. 2017. Web. 19 Sept. 2017.

2. Ibid.

3. "Rainforest Alliance Certified Palm Oil." *Rainforest Alliance*. Rainforest Alliance, 6 June 2016. Web. 19 Sept. 2017.

4. "Conflict Palm Oil." *Rainforest Action Network*. RAN, n.d. Web. 19 Sept. 2017.

5. Alina Bradford. "Deforestation: Facts, Causes & Effects." *LiveScience*. LiveScience, 4 Mar. 2015. Web. 19 Sept. 2017.

6. "Rainforest Alliance Certified Palm Oil." *Rainforest Alliance*. Rainforest Alliance, 6 June 2016. Web. 19 Sept. 2017.

7. Chris Lang. "Oil Palm Plantations Replacing Forests in Kalimantan." *REDD Monitor*. REDD Monitor, 10 Oct. 2012. Web. 19 Sept. 2017.

8. Doug Boucher, et al. "Deforestation Success Stories." *Union of Concerned Scientists*. Union of Concerned Scientists, 2014. Web. 19 Sept. 2017.

9. Ibid. 36–38.

10. "Success—Nigeria: Governor Partly Repeals Ekuri Land Grab." *Rainforest Rescue*. Rainforest Rescue, 17 Feb. 2017. Web. 19 Sept. 2017.

11. Doug Boucher, et al. "Deforestation Success Stories." *Union of Concerned Scientists*. Union of Concerned Scientists, 2014. Web. 19 Sept. 2017.

12. "Congo Basin." *WWF*. WWF, 2017. Web. 19 Sept. 2017.

13. Matthew Warren. "Tropical Peatlands of Southeast Asia: Functions, Threats, and the Role of Fire in Climate Change Mitigation." *UF/IFAS*. University of Florida Institute of Food and Agricultural Sciences, n.d. Web. 19 Sept. 2017.

14. Mike Gaworecki. "World's Largest Tropical Peatlands Discovered in Swamp Forests of Congo Basin." *Mongabay*. Mongabay, 9 Feb. 2017. Web. 19 Sept. 2017.

15. Matthew Warren. "Tropical Peatlands of Southeast Asia: Functions, Threats, and the Role of Fire in Climate Change Mitigation." *UF/IFAS*. University of Florida Institute of Food and Agricultural Sciences, n.d. Web. 19 Sept. 2017.

16. Mike Gaworecki. "World's Largest Tropical Peatlands Discovered in Swamp Forests of Congo Basin." *Mongabay*. Mongabay, 9 Feb. 2017. Web. 19 Sept. 2017.

CHAPTER 5. RESTORATION BY REFORESTATION

1. Eric Ofori. "Mainly Exotic Trees Are Used for Reforestation of Rainforests in Africa." *Nature Today*. Nature Today, 30 Dec. 2015. Web. 19 Sept. 2017.

2. Doug Boucher, et al. "Deforestation Success Stories." *Union of Concerned Scientists*. Union of Concerned Scientists, 2014. Web. 19 Sept. 2017.

3. Ibid. 21–24.

4. "Indonesia Reforestation Project." *Mitsui Sumitomo Insurance*. Mitsui Sumitomo Insurance, n.d. Web. 19 Sept. 2017.

5. Doug Boucher, et al. "Deforestation Success Stories." *Union of Concerned Scientists*. Union of Concerned Scientists, 2014. Web. 19 Sept. 2017.

6. "Indonesia Rainforest Facts." *Orangutan Foundation International*. Orangutan Foundation International, 2017. Web. 19 Sept. 2017.

7. "Indonesia. The Spread and Enlargement of the 'Green Wall.' News from the Field." Conservation International, Aug. 2016. *Daikin Global*. Web. 19 Sept. 2017.

8. "Area de Conservación Guanacaste, Costa Rica." *Southeastern Louisiana University*. Southeastern Louisiana University, n.d. Web. 19 Sept. 2017.

9. "Plant for the Planet: Billion Tree Campaign." *UN and Climate Change*. UN, 12 Aug. 2014. Web. 19 Sept. 2017.

CHAPTER 6. CONSERVING BY PRESERVING

1. Stuart Chape, et al. "2003 United Nations List of Protected Areas." *World Conservation Union*. UNEP World Conservation Monitoring Centre, 2003. Web. 19 Sept. 2017.

2. "Dr. Jane Goodall Teaches Conservation." *MasterClass*. MasterClass, 2017. Web. 19 Sept. 2017.

3. "Central Amazon Conservation Complex." *UNESCO*. UNESCO, 2017. Web. 19 Sept. 2017.

4. "Dr. Jane Goodall Teaches Conservation." *MasterClass*. MasterClass, 2017. Web. 19 Sept. 2017.

5. "Central Amazon Conservation Complex." *UNESCO*. UNESCO, 2017. Web. 19 Sept. 2017.

6. "Jaguar: The Amazon's Amazing Swimming Cat." *WWF-UK*. WWF-UK, n.d. Web. 19 Sept. 2017.

7. "Rainforest: Start Your Expedition." *PBS*. PBS, n.d. Web. 19 Sept. 2017.

8. Ethan Shaw. "The Biggest Forests in Africa." *USA Today*. USA Today, n.d. Web. 19 Sept. 2017.

9. Jesse Lewis. "How We're Saving Madagascar's Most Endangered Species by Protecting Rainforests." *Rainforest Trust*. One Green Planet, 28 July 2017. Web. 19 Sept. 2017.

10. Bonobo Conservation Initiative. "Save Endangered Bonobos in the Congo Rainforest." *Global Giving*. Global Giving, 2017. Web. 19 Sept. 2017.

11. Paul Steyn. "Finding More Ammo Than Animals in Huge African Rain Forest." *National Geographic*. National Geographic Partners, 17 June 2015. Web. 19 Sept. 2017.

12. Ibid.

13. Irina Bright. "Mountain Gorillas: Amongst the Rarest of All Animals." *Tropical Rainforest Animals*. Tropical Rainforest Animals, Jan. 2008. Web. 19 Sept. 2017.

14. "Success – 265,000 Signatures Help Save Pangolins." *Rainforest Rescue*. Rainforest Rescue, 4 Oct. 2016. Web. 19 Sept. 2017.

15. "Dry Forest Ecology." *Ceiba Foundation for Tropical Conservation*. Ceiba Foundation for Tropical Conservation, n.d. Web. 19 Sept. 2017.

16. Ibid.

17. Ibid.

CHAPTER 7. OUTSIDE HELP AND COOPERATION

1. "Responsible Food Systems." *Rainforest Action Network*. RAN, n.d. Web. 19 Sept. 2017.

2. Rhett Butler. "International Rainforest Conservation Organizations." *Mongabay*. Mongabay, 11 July 2012. Web. 19 Sept. 2017.

3. "Congo Basin." *WWF*. WWF, 2017. Web. 19 Sept. 2017.

4. Ian McIntosh. "Ecotourism: A Boon for Indigenous People?" *Cultural Survival Quarterly Magazine*. Cultural Survival, June 1999. Web. 19 Sept. 2017.

CHAPTER 8. THE FUTURE OF TROPICAL FORESTS

1. Rhett Butler. "How to Save Tropical Rainforests." *Mongabay*. Mongabay, 22 July 2017. Web. 19 Sept. 2017.

2. S. Joseph Wright. "The Future of Tropical Forests." *Annals of the New York Academy of Sciences* 1195(May 2010): 1–27. *Research Gate*. Web. 19 Sept. 2017.

3. Scott Mori. "The Future of Tropical Forests in the New World." *New York Botanical Garden*. NYBG, 24 Jan. 2013. Web. 19 Sept. 2017.

4. "World Population Projected to Reach 9.6 Billion by 2050—UN Report." *UN News Centre*. UN News Centre, 13 June 2013. Web. 19 Sept. 2017.

5. "Current World Population." *Worldometers*. Worldometers, n.d. Web. 19 Sept. 2017.

6. Nathaneal Johnson. "48 Hours that Changed the Future of Rainforests." *Grist*. Grist, 2 Apr. 2015. Web. 19 Sept. 2017.

7. Justin Gillis. "Restored Forests Breathe Life into Efforts Against Climate Change." *New York Times*. New York Times, 23 Dec. 2014. Web. 19 Sept. 2017.

8. Ibid.

INDEX

ABOUT THE
AUTHOR

Carol Hand has a PhD in zoology with a specialization in marine ecology and a special interest in environmental and climate science. Before becoming a science writer, she taught college, wrote for standardized testing companies, and developed multimedia science curricula. She has written more than 40 books for young people, including many on science and environmental topics.